NEVER MIND THE JONESES

Building Core Christian Values
in a Way That Fits Your Family

TIM STAFFORD

InterVarsity Press
Downers Grove, Illinois

For a free group discussion guide to this book go to
www.ivpress.com/bookdiscussionguides

InterVarsity Press
P.O. Box 1400, Downers Grove, IL 60515-1426
World Wide Web: www.ivpress.com
E-mail: mail@ivpress.com

InterVarsity Press® is the book-publishing division of InterVarsity Christian Fellowship/USA®, a student movement active on campus at hundreds of universities, colleges and schools of nursing in the United States of America, and a member movement of the International Fellowship of Evangelical Students. For information about local and regional activities, write Public Relations Dept., InterVarsity Christian Fellowship/USA, 6400 Schroeder Rd., P.O. Box 7895, Madison, WI 53707-7895, or visit the IVCF website at <www.ivcf.org>.

All Scripture quotations, unless otherwise indicated, are taken from the Holy Bible, New International Version®. NIV®. Copyright ©1973, 1978, 1984 by International Bible Society. Used by permission of Zondervan Publishing House. All rights reserved.

Cover design: Cindy Kiple

Cover images: family holding hands—Larry Bray/Getty Images; rooftops—Alan Thorton/Getty Images

ISBN 0-8308-3201-7

Printed in Canada ∞

Library of Congress Cataloging-in-Publication Data

Stafford, Tim.
  Never mind the Joneses: building core Christian values in a way that
fits your family/Tim Stafford.
    p. cm.
  ISBN 0-8308-3201-7
  1. Family—Religious life. 2. Family—Religious
  asapects—Christianity. 3. Parenting—Religious aspects—Christianity.
  I. Title.
    BV4526.3.S7 2004
    248.4—dc22

                                                          2003020594

P	18	17	16	15	14	13	12	11	10	9	8	7	6	5	4	3	2	1
Y	18	17	16	15	14	13	12	11	10	09	08	07	06	05	04			

CONTENTS

ACKNOWLEDGMENTS

The thoughts in this book come as much from my wife, Popie, as from me. As partners we have raised our three children, and during the child-rearing years we spent many long, searching hours talking about them and their growth. I could not say where her ideas about family end and mine begin. We have shared everything.

Over a good many years Popie and I have given seminars about family life, developing the core material you will read in this book. Popie is a marriage and family therapist. She has seen hundreds if not thousands of families professionally over the years. Thus her wisdom and professional experience lie behind much of the material in this book. She has read every word of the manuscript many times at different stages of its development, correcting many faults and adding ideas liberally.

Given that history, both of our names might naturally belong on the cover of this book. Popie did not want that. She prefers to keep our professions separate: I am the writer, she the therapist. We share in the contents, but writing it down has been my job. My name is on the cover. Her spirit and wisdom are, I hope, all over the insides.

Several friends read the manuscript and gave very helpful suggestions. Harold Fickett and Philip Yancey, two of the finest writers and editors I know, made many detailed and helpful suggestions. Jim and Mandy Bankson, Gary and Marlene Van Brocklin, and Steve and Kirsten Carpenter gave a careful reading and added their thoughts. I am grateful to them all.

I will not try to name the many friends and family members who have contributed to this book by their good example. I would only mention my own parents, Chase and Harriette Stafford, who made a wonderful marriage and lived out the values I would wish to be known for. I would also mention Popie's parents, Henry and Ozzie Belle Herrod, who have showed profound love for each other and their family.

Special thanks go to Andy Le Peau and the whole team at IVP, who have not forsaken their love for books even though they work in publishing. They are good at what they do, and they make it a pleasure to do it with them. I hope not to disappoint them for the faith they have placed in me.

In these pages I describe a number of families. In order to protect privacy I have sometimes merged different examples or changed details of their story. My intention was to keep the spirit of their example but to disguise their identity so that no one could guess who I had in mind.

Tim Stafford

INTRODUCTION

Parents are besieged with opportunities for their children. Should you enroll Sylvia in gymnastics? or ballet? Latin? or all three? Nobody can decide for you, and no answer is right or wrong. Multiply the decision by a thousand times, though, and it has huge implications.

Even more importantly, how will you raise Sylvia to know subjects for which she cannot enroll? Lots of families produce good gymnasts, good violinists and good students who really have no sense of what it means to love God and to serve other people.

In the urgent confusion of our modern world, parents need a framework for evaluating their choices. Even more, they need an approach that keeps the good from crowding out the best.

This book shows how to put core Christian values at the center of your family life, to make a foundation under sports, music, school and everything else. Core values don't get taught through a lecture. They are caught, on a day-by-day basis, through activities as much as words. This book will show you how to do that in your family. We willtake one value at a time, for fourteen chapters. We'll consider values like truthfulness, hard work and family unity. What are you currently doing that teaches this value? How can you emphasize or strengthen it? Do you need to try something new? And what habits do you need to eliminate?

I am not going to give an exact recipe for family life, because I believe strongly that every family should find its own unique approach. Rather, I'll show you how other families integrate these core values into daily life—lots of different families, in lots of different ways.

ROOTS AND WINGS

"There are two lasting bequests we can give our children. One is roots. The other is wings." I'm not sure who first said that, but the phrase "roots and wings" has been quoted universally—on greeting cards, book jackets and educational programs.

Everybody knows that roots and wings are an unlikely combination. Wings don't grow on trees. Nor do roots and wings come together spontaneously in family life. Only with difficulty do parents teach their children responsibility and yet offer them freedom.

At one extreme, some parents become extremely controlling. They have a clearly defined sense of right and wrong, often prompted by the Bible. Knowing what God expects, how can they fail to insist on obedience in their family? And yet their children, even if they are compliant, may not truly accept their parents' values for their own. If these values aren't integrated into the inner self of the child, then the values will get dumped in college or in the working world, as soon as the children gain some individual freedom.

At the other extreme are parents who provide few boundaries or guidelines for their children. They want their children to be free to find themselves, free not to copy anybody else. Yet their children often grow up without any real sense of guidance. With no core values, they may fall prey to the easier values of a material culture—money, appearance, status or style. They become not liberated but lost.

The framework of this book provides both roots and wings. Roots come from core values found in Scripture. Add these core values together and you have a portrait of life lived well. Is there a parent who doesn't want this for his or her children?

FAMILY CULTURE

The wings of grace come from what I call "family culture." I'll explain this idea in more detail later. For the present let me simply say that family culture is the answer to the question, "What makes your family different from every other?" Families have rituals, habits and traditions that mix together in a way that belongs uniquely to them. Each family develops its own style and its own flavor.

You value friendliness? Your family culture will show it. You value simplicity? money? education? extended family? Your family culture expresses your values.

Family culture can flex to fit the people you are. It expresses your creativity and personality. Family culture can be your "wings."

This book will help you sort through each of fourteen core values and consider how to integrate them in your family culture. I'll give lots of examples to demonstrate how one value can take many forms, depending on the family. You have lots of possibilities. The important point is, choose one. Or more than one!

The result is a paradox. In one sense, if you claim to be a Christian family, you have the same ambitions as every other Christian family. You don't need to be creative about values. You already have the God-given best.

Paradoxically, though, the way you live out those values will make you unlike any other family on the face of the earth.

There is a simple explanation for this paradox. It is rooted in the character of God. He loves goodness. He also loves variety. (Look at the universe he made.) Therefore he wants his people to show both.

A DEEPER KIND OF GRACE

With deepest concern I want to add that our families need another kind of grace: the grace to forgive ourselves. I hope this kind of grace will show through every line of this book.

A danger lurks in core values. They must be lived with a light touch. That lightness is the touch of grace. A family may have all the right values and live them out with rigor, but if the family lacks grace and forgiveness their home will be oppressive and lifeless. From the outside that may not be obvious. From the inside it will throw up powerful emotional responses.

Our children come into the world capable of great good and equally capable of becoming lost and futile. We can train them toward the light, but they are quite able to choose another way. We would not want our children to be anything but free. Their freedom, however, can break our hearts.

That is why we pray for our children. We know that even if we were perfect parents, our children would need more than our perfection could offer. And we are very far from perfect parents.

I know parents who have done their best and now feel disappointed, worried and sometimes guilty. The parents may feel angry with themselves for failing their children, or angry with the children for failing to live up to the good life they were taught.

"Man's anger does not bring about the righteous life that God desires" (James 1:20). Anger is futile; only God's grace and forgiveness has the power to change us for the better. I think that is why the Bible tells us relatively little about how to be an ideal parent—and a great deal about how to live by God's grace. This book is dedicated to good parenting, and I hope that it will help many families to raise good children. The best parenting, though, comes from our Father in heaven.

> He does not treat us as our sins deserve
> or repay us according to our iniquities.
> For as high as the heavens are above the earth,
> so great is his love for those who fear him;
> as far as the east is from the west,
> so far has he removed our transgressions from us.
> As a father has compassion on his children,
> so the LORD has compassion on those who fear him.
> (Psalm 103:10-13)

May such grace penetrate our skins and get all the way into our hearts.

1

FAMILY CULTURE
There Is Nobody Like You

I grew up in Fresno, a city in the hot, dry agricultural heart of California. Fresno is quite unlike the beaches-and-bridges California you see on television. It is flat, sprawling and unsophisticated, a drowsy and unbeautiful cow town. The weather is awful. Fresno has a saving grace, however. A few miles out of town the foothills of the Sierra Nevada Mountains rise out of the plain. Stay on the road and soon you enter the cool ranges of Yosemite, Kings Canyon and Sequoia National Parks.

In junior high school I began to hike these mountains with my dad and my friend Murray. Every summer the jagged, snow-streaked high country drew us into weeks of backpacking. For our "long trips" we went two weeks on the trail, never seeing a road, traversing mile after mile of high, rugged mountain country. I loved it like nothing else I did. I found freedom, challenge, peace and beauty. To this day I get slightly giddy on my way into the high mountains.

When I married Popie Herrod, she joined me in this love. We traipsed many wonderful trails in our first years together. Naturally, when we had children, we wanted to take them backpacking too. We restrained ourselves until our youngest was old enough to hike, and then we began to introduce all three kids to short trips. We tried (not always successfully) to make our hikes easy and fun.

Our oldest, Katie, did not take to it. At that point in her life she had little use for exercise. We used to joke that her idea of a workout was making her bed. She felt no enthusiasm for carrying a pack, sleeping in tents or digging a hole to go to the bathroom. She had problems with altitude sickness.

Her disaffection reached a peak one summer day south of Mt. Whit-
ney. Katie was about twelve then. A wild afternoon storm caught us as
our trail wound along the side of a very high ridge, just at timberline.
Rain poured down in sheets; lightning bolts crashed among the sparse
trees. As rain saturated the sandy ground, thick flows of soil and water
surged across our trail. The whole mountain seemed ready to come apart
under our feet.

I went ahead as fast as I could, seeking a place to put up our tents.
Popie stayed with Katie. She was throwing-up sick, wet and miserable.
Tears streamed down her face. "I hate this!" she cried. "I hate it, I hate it,
I hate it! And the thing I hate the most is that I know when I grow up
I'm going to marry someone just like Dad, and we'll make *our* kids go
backpacking!"

Ten years have passed since that memorable day. Katie survived the
rainstorm. She survived other backpacking trips too. She is now a college graduate, and—what do you know?—she has become a fairly enthusiastic backpacker. As I write, she is spending her summer as a cook
at a Yosemite High Sierra Camp, hiking long distances on her days off.
It remains to be seen how accurate her prophecy will turn out to be—
whether she will marry a backpacker and force her kids to hike—but so
far, so good.

Family culture works like that. Backpacking is part of who the
Staffords are. At some level, even while retching in a downpour, Katie
knew that. Family culture has great strength to perpetuate itself. I
would be little surprised to find my grandchildren's grandchildren hiking into the wilderness with packs on their backs. We're talking about
Staffords, aren't we?

The Staffords are hardly alone in passing on their peculiarities. Because of family culture, generations of adults find themselves giving their
children exactly the same lecture (on homework, on manners, on boy-
friends and girlfriends) that they remember hearing from their parents—
a lecture they may have hated at the time.

Because of family culture, some families always play cards or board
games on their summer vacations.

Because of family culture, millions of dads grow unaccountably misty-eyed while they watch a five-year-old son unwrap a baseball glove (or a football, or a soccer ball, or a basketball) for Christmas.

Because of family culture, some households have never allowed a ketchup bottle on the dining room table.

Because of family culture, some families always have diet soda in the fridge.

Because of family culture, some families read a passage of the Bible over breakfast every morning.

Because of family culture, some young parents begin to think warmly about Sunday school when their children become toddlers, even though the parents themselves haven't attended church in years.

And so on. The great novelist Leo Tolstoy began *Anna Karenina* with this famous line: "Happy families are all alike; every unhappy family is unhappy in its own way." Tolstoy thus revealed that he knew nothing about happy families. Happy families, just as much as unhappy families, are gloriously different from each other. They carry on unique traditions and habits, so that each family in the world is distinct from every other. Children absorb these traditions and habits almost without knowing it, which is one reason why marriage comes as such a shock. Newly married people soon find out that the way they always did it at home is, according to their new life partner, downright weird.

I remember, for instance, discovering that Popie could not tolerate eating from a plate placed directly on a table, without a place mat or tablecloth in between. In her family, place mats were as basic as oxygen. In my family, place mats hardly existed. I thought they were a big waste of time. Guess who prevailed? Now Popie and I always eat off place mats. Our children have rarely eaten from a plate placed directly on a table. Place mats are part of our family culture.

Family culture should not be confused with family traditions. Family traditions include practices like reading the Christmas story on Christmas Eve, watching the annual Big Game at Grandma's house or making Velvet Chocolate birthday cakes. Traditions make up part of family culture, but family culture is larger. It embraces everything we

do, even (especially?) practices we follow without realizing we are doing anything peculiar.

In some families, you're expected to leave the room if you lose your
temper. In other families, arriving late to events is absolutely forbidden.
Do you think these families articulate these rules? Usually they have
passed them on unconsciously, as part of family culture. It takes an out-
sider to notice and point out that what "everybody does" isn't necessarily
what everybody does.

Some families have lots of traditions, and some have very few. All families have lots of family culture. Family culture is simply the particular,
peculiar way you do things in your family—everything from how you
celebrate the New Year to how you make lunch.

WHO'S RIGHT, WHO'S WRONG?

I first began to think about family culture when, as a young father, I noticed that some very fine families—friends of mine—approached parenting quite differently than Popie and I did.

From the first day of our marriage, Popie and I took family life seriously. But so did the Joneses. We knew them well, and we respected their
commitment. Why, then, did they do things so differently from us? They
home-schooled their children; ours attended public schools. They lis-
tened to Christian radio; we tuned in to NPR. While a local church was
our lifeblood, the Joneses switched from one church to another and
didn't press their kids to attend youth group.

The Joneses ran a tight ship. Every family member had chores and responsibilities and schedules. Perhaps because Popie and I both worked
at jobs with flexible schedules, we were more supple, not to say downright slack.

As a family the Joneses always dressed well, while as teenagers our
kids thought the Salvation Army thrift store was a cool place to buy
clothes. We drove our cars until they died (and they were usually clut-
tered with old papers). The Joneses leased, and I'll let you guess how
clean they kept their cars.

Our disciplinary styles were different too. Even though the Joneses lived by a strict regimen, they put up with whining I could never stand. When the Jones children were toddlers, they seemed like terrible brats to me. I noticed, though, that when they got a little older they turned out to have perfectly good manners.

I like the Joneses, and I enjoy their company, but I wouldn't want to be a member of their family. I like my family the way it is. I like the way we talk. I like the way we dress. I don't care to worry about how clean my car is.

The Joneses live *differently*. Does that make our way right and theirs wrong? Or vice versa—should I feel guilty because I don't live up to some of their standards? I don't think so. Most of our differences have to do with taste and style, not right and wrong.

I began to think that there might be more than one good way to raise a family.

As far as core values are concerned, I am sure we agree with the Joneses almost 100 percent. We believe in the same God, and our senses of right and wrong are virtually identical. We could go through a list of family values and agree on every one. When it comes to living out those values, however, we have different approaches.

The Joneses have their reasons for living the way they do. So do we. We could discuss our differences, but at the end of the discussion we might still disagree. They believe their approach will be more successful at raising children with values. We believe *our* approach will be more successful. Actually, we might both be successful. It appears to me that, in the end, the Staffords will produce more Staffords, while the Joneses will produce more Joneses.

CULTURE EXPRESSES VALUES

As a young married couple, Popie and I lived in Kenya, East Africa, for several years. Talk about cultural differences! Not only did we live differently from most Africans, we learned that Africans live very differently from each other.

Popie taught a college class in marriage and family. She would encourage students—who came from countries all over the continent—

to tell about their family customs. Most Africans, like most Americans, assume that people who look like them practice marriage and family the same way. Amazement and consternation came as they learned, for example, that some Africans hold matrilineal rather than patrilineal traditions. "Are you telling me that your sister is the one to inherit the family land?" Some of them could hardly believe what they heard from fellow Africans.

Living with different cultures, you learn that your way of doing things is not the only way. For example, when we first got to Nairobi we met charming people at church and at other gatherings, people who seemed to like us and with whom we thought we could cultivate friendship. When we tried to invite them to our home for dinner, though, something went wrong. Our would-be friends said yes, yes, that would be lovely, but they didn't seem to want to be pinned down. If we insisted on setting a date they got out their calendars but somehow found it almost impossible to locate an open evening. The process was oddly uncomfortable. Once or twice we thought we had agreed on a date but when the time came, nobody showed up. Since we didn't have a phone—nor did most people in those days in Nairobi—we couldn't call to see what the trouble was.

We began to think that making friends with Kenyans was all but impossible. They appeared to be friendly people, but we could never get beyond superficial chats after church.

Finally in exasperation we point-blank asked a Kenyan couple what we were doing wrong. They laughed. "If you want to make friends with people, you don't invite them to your house," they said. "You go to theirs."

"That would be fine," we said, "but they haven't invited us."

"No, they don't invite you. You just go."

"Without any warning? What if they already have guests? What if they are about to have dinner?"

"Oh, that would be even better!"

The first time we knocked at the door of some people we hardly knew, without any invitation, my nerves were stretched tight. As soon as the door opened, however, I saw that we had done the right thing. They welcomed us in, they fed us, they talked to us like the best of friends. They were obviously delighted to see us. And then they started coming to *our* house unannounced.

Kenyans have their own way of practicing hospitality. It works just fine for them. Americans have a different way. It works pretty well for us. One is not right and one is not wrong. What is right is the value of hospitality.

THE MEANING OF CULTURE

This brings me to a fundamental definition, one I will rely on throughout the rest of this book.

Culture is habitual ways of life transmitting values into practical living.

Culture is habit. Culture includes the ways of life that we hardly know we do. We just do them. Culture is turkey on Thanksgiving. You cook a turkey because that is your habitual way of life. Turkey is not morally superior to lasagna. Turkey on Thanksgiving is simply what we do. You don't have to ask what is on the menu. Turkey is always on the menu.

Culture transmits values. Behind every cultural habit there's a value statement, however slight. Sometimes you have to think awhile to understand what the value is, but values always are inherent in culture.

We eat turkey at Thanksgiving because a turkey is a big bird that feeds a lot of people. The turkey celebrates abundance, and it expresses our commitment to sharing our enjoyment of abundance with extended family and community. We could say the same thing in words. We could even put it in a mission statement. The turkey says it better.

Culture transmits values into practical living. Culture creates a living parable to pass on values for the next generation. From family culture, children learn values before they can even talk. And they don't forget them. Habits stick, where mission statements may soon be forgotten.

NEVER MIND ABOUT THE JONESES

When two people get married, they pick a little of the husband's family culture, a little of the wife's. They throw in something from the neighbors. They add their hobbies and interests, their personalities and ideals. They are influenced by what they admire on TV and the movies, and also by what region of the country they live in. A church may play a part—not just what is preached, but what the young couples group talks about.

When children come along, they drastically influence the family culture. You may think that you are shaping children, but they also shape you. From birth, children are who they are: shy or outgoing, athletic or sedentary, stubborn or easygoing. If you are blessed with boys who think, as my son Chase did, that all the important forces in the universe are summed up in a bouncing ball, you can plan on wrapping your family culture around sports. If you are blessed with girls like my daughter Katie, loving art and drama and playing with dolls, expect another kind of family culture. (I need hardly add that girls may love games and boys may love drama.)

Stir all the various factors together, and you create the unique flavor that sets the Staffords and the Joneses apart from every other family.

Family culture creates the wonderful sense of relaxation we get inside our own four walls. Family culture gives family vacations their wonderful, inexplicable pleasure. (Even the disasters are *our* disasters.) Here, and only here in the heart of the family, does everybody understand. Here we have a sense of freedom to be just who we are.

Of course, family culture can also drive you crazy. Mostly, though, family culture is like a ten-year-old mutt. He's comfortable and comforting. He may be old, he may be ugly, but he's ours.

The question is, can the mutt be trained?

2
CORE VALUES
How to Shape Your Family Culture

We live in an era when traditional beliefs have been tossed aside and when popular culture—television, movies and music—displays terribly corrosive morality. Families are much shakier than they used to be. You can no longer assume—if you ever could—that solid values will be passed on from one generation to the next. Building families takes careful, intentional work.

A generation ago Americans could believe that, just growing up in the neighborhood, children would absorb some fundamental standards. Parents sent their kids to play next door serene in the faith that their neighbors would reinforce their values. They sent their children off to school confident that teachers and administrators believed more or less as they did. Raising children with values is not so easy anymore. Neighborhoods and schools contain people with a wide variety of moral beliefs, many of which would horrify my grandparents. Meanwhile, right in the living room of almost every home is a television, broadcasting hours of imaginative programs that evidence few signs of enduring values.

This situation worries parents tremendously. They feel responsible to give their children a strong moral upbringing, yet to do so they sometimes must stand apart from their neighbors. It's not the easiest position. People look around for help and support.

All sorts of organizations have responded to the crisis of family values—foundations, youth organizations, churches, synagogues, even government commissions. The response is a mixed bag, good and bad. Sometimes it seems puny in the face of the cultural tide. Nevertheless, families can find help and support that didn't exist a generation ago.

Think how the Christian scene has changed. When my parents were young, Christian conferences and radio programs (there were no TV programs, religious or secular) concentrated almost exclusively on doctrine and Bible. Nowadays they give nearly equal chunks of time to marriage and family. Many books and magazines offer guidance. Christian psychologists, once almost unknown, have become prominent leaders. Churches offer counseling and classes on parenting.

Is it enough? Judging by the results, I don't think so. Our situation remains troubled, and families continue to look for help.

In the previous chapter I made the case that each family has its own unique culture, and that family culture transmit values into daily living. I'm convinced family culture is the single most powerful force for passing on values. I'm also convinced that we overlook its potential to help parents.

Consider one classic value: hard work. Parents worry about whether their children learn this value, and for good reason. Clearly some never do. How can we teach the next generation how to work? Here's one approach: we could start Institutes of Hard Work, which offer summer seminars for young people. We could develop a special one-semester course, required for high school graduation, to study the importance of work and to pass on key skills for hard workers. We could fund public service advertisements, flooding the airwaves and billboards with a special appeal: "Work: It's Good for Everyone." Academic studies, pilot programs and scholarship essay-writing contests might also contribute.

I venture that none of these approaches would accomplish nearly so much as the venerable "chore chart" posted on the refrigerator and enforced by parental rewards and punishments. Parents who want their children to know the value of hard work must develop a family culture of hard work. They may have to stop playing golf on Saturdays so they have time to work alongside their children at home projects, such as putting in an irrigation system or setting a brick sidewalk. Alternatively, they can go as a family to volunteer at a Habitat home-build every Saturday. Lots of different approaches can be made to suit families' varied needs, as we'll see in chapter five. By whatever approach, family culture teaches values sooner and better than government institutes, school require-ments or any number of lectures and threats.

THE IMPORTANCE OF FREEDOM

Furthermore, family culture is a flexible tool. Flexibility matters, because it offers freedom.

I'm concerned with one-size-fits-all parenting advice. It doesn't mat-ter whether the advice is liberal or conservative. If one family home-schools, they want everybody to home-school. If one family experiences success letting children set their own mealtimes, they propose that ev-erybody do the same. If one family trains the children to address adults as Mr., Mrs. or Miss, they think fellow church members should follow their lead.

Family culture says: Yes, those may be valid and helpful ways to ex-press values. They aren't the only ways, though. Go around the world and see how different people in different places and different cultures raise children. Go from family to family. You'll find many ways of edu-cating children, many ways of structuring meals, many ways for children to show respect for adults. The goals may be the same, but different cul-tures take different routes to arrive at the same end point.

I want to raise my children so that they absorb core values, but I very much want to do it in a way that offers freedom. Sometimes we feel pres-sured to adopt an approach that suits the Joneses but doesn't really fit the kind of people *we* are. When that happens, our kids may rebel. What's more, our neighbors may feel cut off from us. They sense the judgmentalism implicit in our approach. They're not sure they want to follow our footsteps, if that means walking in lockstep.

When Paul wrote to the Galatian church, he noted that they had once been a joyful congregation. "You were running a good race. Who cut in on you?" (Galatians 5:7). Apparently a group of very zealous Christians convinced them that there existed only one way to live as a Christian, the Jewish way, following Old Testament traditions. Paul replied pas-sionately, "It is for freedom that Christ has set us free" (5:1)!

Family culture facilitates that freedom. Family culture enables us to pass on core values while honoring our individual personalities—our quirks, our personal preferences, our interests and temperaments.

CORE VALUES

Not all family values are good. Family culture can transmit materialism, as when families compete for who can give the most extravagant gifts. Family culture can transmit cutthroat competition, as when they make winning at cards an obsession. Family culture can pass on racism, meanness or an obsession with appearance. It can transmit the ways in which some men dominate women and some women dominate men.

Most of us grew up in families that practiced at least a few unwholesome values. If we drift along, we may perpetuate those. We may also drift into conformity with a demoralized culture.

I'm proposing that we shape our family cultures, systematically thinking them through, strengthening what has value and changing what does not.

To help do that, I've gone through the Bible looking for core values. Starting with the Ten Commandments, I went on to consider the sermons of the prophets, Paul's letters, and Jesus' teachings, particularly the Sermon on the Mount. I considered the wisdom literature, especially Proverbs and James. Wherever the Bible offered ethical teaching, I tried to think about the underlying values.

I came up with fourteen core values, which I believe include all God's fundamental ethical expectations as they are described in the Bible. I admit that another student of Scripture might enumerate these values somewhat differently. Some values might be split in two; others could be combined or given another name. Any time you try to give a brief summary of the Bible's teaching, you make arguable choices. Nevertheless, I believe all Christians (and many people of other faiths too) will recognize this as a summary of essential values. At the beginning of each chapter, I list some key Scriptures that emphasize this value.

1. *God first.* Honoring God comes before anything else.

2. *Concern for others.* Jesus told us to love our neighbors as we love our-

selves. That means constantly and scrupulously paying attention to their welfare. Included in "concern for others" are matters like evangelism and justice.

3. *Hard work.* Whatever we work at, we should do wholeheartedly. We work not just to please ourselves but also to please God and all those to whom we are responsible.

4. *Truthfulness.* Our words should be filled with truth, and no words that undercut the truth.

5. *Generosity.* God wants an overflowing and openhanded love for others, especially in how we invest our possessions.

6. *Submission.* In many different settings—work, marriage, church, government—we fit into a larger scheme and submit to the leadership of someone else. Submission implies accepting our limited role in the world.

7. *Sexual fidelity.* Faithfulness to a marriage partner implies eliminating anything that interferes with our love for that partner. Single people express sexual faithfulness by living chaste lives.

8. *Family unity and love.* The family is a core unit that demands respect, support and love. So does the church, as God's family.

9. *Boundaries.* God has given each individual certain areas of responsibility that belong to him or her alone. First is his or her body. Next is his or her property. Jobs, family and relationships may also be private. These areas of individual responsibility should be protected. Theft, sexual harassment and gossip are some of the sins that violate these boundaries.

10. *Joy and thanksgiving.* Celebration should be part of every day, because we recognize all that God does for us.

11. *Rest.* We work within the limits of the time and ability God has given us. After working, we need to stop for renewal.

12. *Care for creation.* God made humans responsible to develop and care for all that he has created. Harmony, not destruction, should mark the interaction between human development and the rest of God's creation.

13. *Contentment*. With whatever we have and whatever we are, in whatever place or position God has put us, we should learn to be at peace.

14. *Grace*. We are meant to follow in the footsteps of God himself, offering forgiveness and grace to others even when it isn't deserved.

CORE VALUES: THE BUILDING CODE OF FAMILY LIFE

These core values form the basic architecture of family life. Think of them
like a building code. In any American community, a builder has to abide
by detailed codes. As a result, every house, big or small, low-budget or
luxury, follows the same basic standards. If you climb under the house,
you see the same plumbing, the same conduit, the same insulation, the
same width between studs. But what a world of difference in the homes
created under these codes! The same basic construction techniques can
be used to create a California ranchette or a neo-Victorian mansion. The
wildest imagination of architects and homeowners gets expressed.

How do you build out core values? Every family must decide that for
themselves—prayerfully, thoughtfully, even experimentally. Sometimes
you have to try things to see how they work for you.

Parents begin the process, when kids are small. As children grow
older they can be included in the process.

Even the way you decide is up to you. Some families are good at meetings. Their family culture includes discussion and debate. They can use-
fully spend Monday evenings working through this list of core values,
thrashing out how to live them out. For other families, meetings are
painful. Maybe it works better to offer a really juicy prize to the family
member who comes up with the best idea for incorporating a core value.

However they approach it, families can use the fourteen core values
as a framework for thinking through family life. For one way of taking
inventory, you may want look ahead to "A Few Final Words" at the end
of the book. There I give a sample approach drawn from my family.

THE BROKENNESS OF FAMILIES

When I talked to my friend John about my idea for this book, he said, "I
know what my first response would be—guilt. Any time I hear someone

talk about core values I should live by, I'm thinking of all the ways I've failed."

He meant it. Some people—a lot of people—find it excruciatingly painful to discuss family culture, because they feel their intense disappointment and guilt. In this book you will read about many ways that families put their core values into practice. At least a few times you will almost certainly think, *Too late. Too late* is a very depressing thought, when it applies to your children.

We can easily focus on the ways we blew it. And we did all blow it. No perfect families exist. In fact, most families I know feel that they're barely surviving. How can you calmly discuss core values when you feel this way? It's like trying to repair a rickety fence in the middle of a hurricane while you have the flu.

If you grew up with yelling, you tend to yell. If you grew up with your mother mistrusting everybody, you tend not to trust anybody. Many people feel that they have passed along bad values to their children—the same bad values they inherited from their parents. It's depressing to see your kids acting the same way, repeating the mistakes and the sins of their uncles and aunts and older brothers and sisters—not to mention their parents.

And what if you're in a difficult marriage? Or what if you've already split from a difficult marriage? What if you're a single parent or a stepparent? Most people find it very difficult to think calmly and hopefully about family culture when they feel deeply unhappy about their own family circumstances. If you and your spouse disagree on basic issues, how can you make joint decisions about family culture? If you're alone, you may wonder where you'll find the time or energy to even think about core values.

Here's one final difficulty. What if you don't really care that much? When you search your heart, you may discover that you're a moral couch potato. Yes, in some theoretical sense you want your family to demonstrate good values, but in reality you don't have the energy and commitment to change.

Concerns like these can paralyze you. They can cause you to quit before you start. Perhaps you don't feel paralyzed, but your husband or wife has these feelings so intensely that he or she can't begin to join you in thinking about family culture.

The world is full of brokenness, and we feel it in our families. In the very same places where some find love, solace and grace, others find despair. It always will be so until a new heaven and earth come and we are renewed through Jesus Christ.

In the meantime, brokenness is not the only reality. We must hold close these counterbalancing realities and hopes.

There is no perfect way, just your way. Many parents feel guilty that they can't stick to strict discipline. They have good intentions, but they're inconsistent. They lose their cool. They give in. They have in mind a perfectly disciplined family life, but they never match it. They feel like failures.

I'm not so sure they should. Families are not machines, and they do not run by invariable rules. Teenagers in particular naturally question and even push back. A good many "strict" homes produce time bombs, ready to go off as soon as they get out of the house. I have heard this story too many times, even from adults who went wild at the age of forty.

Sometimes "strict" breaks down because the system doesn't fit the people who live in it. The system may need adjustment, not the people. Your family may never match the perfect family you know from church. You may never manage to imitate the image you have in your head. That's okay, because that image isn't you—it is only an image. That perfect family from church isn't you either. God knows who you are, and he knows who your kids are. He wants you to find the way that belongs uniquely to you.

God forgives and heals. God is in the healing business every day. Daily he takes our sins and failings to his heart, expunging them from our lives. Daily he offers a new beginning, unstained by yesterday's messes. We need courage to start again, after so many mistakes. God wants to give that courage.

God works for good. A successful family doesn't depend entirely on you, either. God makes it his business to raise families. He is working at it, often in ways you are not aware of. Sometimes you should step back and watch him work. Sometimes you just have to get out of his way.

Our failings do not define our families. You may feel certain that you're too late to fix what is broken, but for God nothing is too late.

Life is not over yet. Regret and disappointment come particularly to parents whose children are grown or whose marriage has already been destroyed. They need to remember the old saying, "While there is life, there is hope." In fact, even in death there is hope. We never know what thoughts and prayers a person takes to the grave.

We can *always* hope. How many people change their lives dramatically when they're middle-aged? How many come back to a faith and a life that they thoroughly rejected when they were young? A lot do. Don't give up hope. Don't stop praying and loving. I have known many families whose lives were redeemed and relationships reconciled very late.

Something is better than nothing. I'll grant you, a list of fourteen core values can intimidate. Some people see only fourteen areas of failure. They feel overwhelmed. They feel that they can't ever manage to live up to such a list. Something is better than nothing, however. If you improve just one small area of family life, you've done something. Start small, begin with the doable, and eventually you may find that you have done more than you expected. In this book you'll learn about dozens of "family habits" that express core values. Pick one.

Don't think the brokenness in your family surprises God or overwhelms him. I guarantee you it does not. God is very familiar with troubled families. He has been dealing with them for a very long time. He is equipped to help restore them, if he can get family members to cooperate. It starts with you. Will you try?

3

GOD FIRST

At the Center of Your Family

"You shall have no other gods before me." EXODUS 20:3

"Love the Lord your God with all your heart and with all your soul and with all your mind." MATTHEW 22:37

"Pray continually." 1 THESSALONIANS 5:17

"Offer your bodies as living sacrifices, holy and pleasing to God." ROMANS 12:1

All genuine Christian believers can remember a time—possibly multiple times—when they decided to put God first. The circumstances vary greatly. Some people remember joining a mass commitment, stepping into a river of sober individuals who streamed to the front of a vast auditorium or stadium. Others remember being quite alone at the moment of decision. Whether they sat in a crowded classroom or wandered a deserted beach, in their thoughts they were alone with God. In their thoughts they gave themselves to him.

Nineteenth-century evangelist Charles Finney described his own conversion vividly. As a skeptical lawyer in western New York, he had been struggling and resisting God for some time when he began to pray.

Without expecting it, without ever having the thought in my mind that there was any such thing for me, without any recollection that

I had ever heard the thing mentioned by any person in the world, at a moment entirely unexpected by me, the Holy Spirit descended upon me in a manner that seemed to go through me, body and soul. I could feel the impression, like a wave of electricity, going through and through me. Indeed it seemed to come in waves, and waves of liquid love—for I could not express it in any other way. And yet it did not seem like water, but rather as the breath of God. I can recollect distinctly that it seemed to fan me, like immense wings; and it seemed to me, as these waves passed over me, that they literally moved my hair like a passing breeze.

No words can express the wonderful love that was shed abroad in my heart. It seemed to me that I should burst. I wept aloud with joy and love and I do not know but I should say I literally *bellowed out* the unutterable gushings of my heart. These waves came over me, and over me, and over me one after the other, until I recollect I cried out, "I shall *die* if these waves continue to pass over me." . . .

How long I continued in this state, with this baptism continuing to roll over me and go through me, I do not know. But I know it was late in the evening when a member of my choir—for I was the leader of the choir—came into the office to see me. He was a member of the church. He found me in this state of loud weeping, and said to me, "Mr. Finney, what ails you?" I could make him no answer for some time. He then said, "Are you in pain?" I gathered up myself as best I could and replied, "No; but I am so happy that I cannot live." (*The Original Memoirs of Charles G. Finney,* pp. 23-24)

At the moment when you feel such happiness, or anything remotely like it, you hardly need the first commandment. Putting God first is a matter of impulse. Finney, on the very day after his conversion, canceled a court case and announced to his disappointed client that he would henceforward work only for Jesus Christ. Though he had been a busy, ambitious lawyer, he felt that law no longer held an interest to him. It was like the moon that disappears when the sun rises. He could only serve God.

Finney's experience was extraordinary, but many people wake up on the day after their conversion hungry to pray, to read Scripture, to tell anybody and everybody about the momentous change.

Nobody, however, stays in that happiness forever. Sooner or later every Christian experiences a loss of ardor. I do not mean a loss of faith. A person can continue to believe just as thoroughly, but the passion dissipates. A sense of humdrum sets in—a feeling that God is wonderful and essential but, after all, life is full of a lot of other things. A person in that state of mind can easily slide into putting job or money or fun ahead of God. Job, money and fun are practical and real; God seems less so. The first commandment becomes more difficult then, and more necessary. Believers enter a soul-struggle, seeking to put God first and to keep him there.

How do you *keep* God first? One approach is to rekindle the fire. Remembering that first (or latest) moment of consecration, believers seek to recreate it. They go to meetings, read devotional literature, pray, fast, confess their struggles to friends. Here I can offer good news: frequently, the effort is rewarded. When people draw near to God, he draws near to them (James 4:8). They understand again what they already knew—the incomparable qualities of God. Once again he claims first place in their lives.

Inevitably, though, this revival also flags. Passion for God comes and goes again, whereas the commandment is constant. The Bible does not say, "Put God first when you feel his presence near." It says, "Love the Lord your God with all your heart and with all your soul and with all your mind." Implied is, "always." We ought to be as constant in our love for God as he is for us.

Because of this, most people—perhaps all who are serious about their faith—get to a second approach: law. *If I make some rules for myself,* we figure, *those rules can keep me pointed toward God.* So, for example, I make a rule for myself to read the Bible and pray when I get up in the morning. I may not feel like it every day. That is exactly the reason why I need to do it every day. I need Scripture's constant reminder of God, because I so easily fall away.

Law certainly can bring problems, particularly if people get their salvation tied up in it. A lot of the apostle Paul's writing deals with exactly this issue. You do meet people plagued with guilt if they forget occasionally to carry through the rules they accepted for themselves. Sometimes very dedicated, serious believers fall into thinking that their relationship with God depends on their flawless behavior. They forget that their salvation comes by God's grace, not their efforts.

In themselves, rules don't have to be oppressive. Rules help people remember to do what is good for them. Brushing your teeth before you go to bed is a useful rule and habit that keeps your teeth from getting cavities. A daily and regular time set aside for prayer, similarly, keeps you pointed in the right direction, reminding you to put God first.

The first commandment is not tyrannical. Difficult to follow, certainly it is. Easy to distort, yes. Yet in the simplest and most profound way, putting God first rewards those who do it. God *is* first. Since he made us and everything that exists, we find our lives rightly oriented when we live according to him. He is the Source of life, the most significant and best out of everything that we ever know. Those who put God first—truly first, not bowing toward their religious emotions or their idea of how a godly person ought to feel—will find him profoundly satisfying. They will find life flowing into them. The experience will draw them back to God, again and again.

THE PROBLEMS OF PREACHING TO YOUR FAMILY

This happy reality—that God is first, and rewards those who seek him first—often gets twisted when Christians apply it to their families. There is a great difference between turning your own attention toward God and trying to get someone else to do the same. My well-meaning attempt to help you may seem to you heavy-handed and oppressive.

A popular term for heavy-handed religion is *fundamentalism.* I realize that fundamentalism began as an attempt to reclaim the "fundamentals" of Christian faith, and that today some people use the word in a particular theological way. My apologies to them, but in popular language—and often in real life—fundamentalism describes a legalistic mindset. A fundamentalist insists that everybody live up to the fundamentalists' set of rules. He or she is often narrow-minded and judgmental, quick to pick out faults in others.

Though it's popular to come down hard on fundamentalists, I'm convinced that they have good intentions. Particularly in raising their children, they don't mean to portray a legalistic faith. They simply want desperately to see their children grow up putting God first.

When you talk to people raised in overly strict homes, however, you often encounter a genuine tragedy. Instead of learning to put God first, these children may learn to resent and fear his demands on their lives. God becomes a tyrant to them.

So some have rebounded in the opposite direction. Whereas fundamentalist families have loads of rules, recent generations have few if any religious commitments at all. In fact, many "liberal" families today believe that no child should be forced to participate in any activity he or she can't authentically embrace. These parents think their duty lies in exposing their children to Christian faith, then getting out of the way so that the children can make up their own minds.

The results are no more encouraging than the results of fundamentalism. Children raised by this liberal approach may not be burdened with guilt, but they very often aren't burdened with God, either. Their parents communicate, effectively, that God is optional. That is a long way from communicating that God is first.

Their mistake is in thinking that they must *give* their children freedom of choice. You cannot give children freedom of choice. God already has! They are born with it, and they will soon figure out how to use it. All parents can do is to give children a Christian upbringing—to help them to see how wonderful life is when lived by God's values.

In other areas, we know this perfectly well. We don't generally "expose" children to the traffic laws, the schools and the habit of brushing teeth, and then let them make up their own minds. In the long run they will certainly make up their own minds, with or without our permission. In the short run, however, we do everything we can to encourage them to obey the laws, go to school and brush their teeth. So why should we not do everything we can to get them to put God first—to grow up with the sweet breeze of God's priority full in their faces?

FAMILY CULTURE

That bring us to family culture—the most powerful tool we have to bring "God first" into the lives of our family. It's not a lecture. It's not a law. It's a way of life.

You could say that family culture was God's approach to teaching the nation of Israel to put him first. Most of the Old Testament rituals were designed to make people's lives revolve around the reality of God. On a regular basis, they had to bring sacrifices to the temple. On a regular basis they participated in national festivals. Even the detailed (and sometimes nearly incomprehensible) ritual laws about what foods to avoid and how to treat skin diseases may seem designed less with health in mind than with God in mind. That is, you had to obey God's law day in and day out, just because you belonged to him, not because you understood the value of what he asked you to do. Why avoid shellfish? Because God's people did, in obedience to him. Observing the command reminded you that you belonged to the God who gave the command.

God gave a long list of "God first" rules to his people in the Old Testament. Those rules don't apply across the board to Christians today. We aren't obligated to sacrifice lambs in the temple, or to avoid shellfish as a sign of belonging to God. Some activities remain clearly out of bounds—idolatry, fornication, human sacrifice, for example. On the whole, though, we have freedom through God's Spirit to make "God first" part of our daily life's fabric, and to do it in our own way.

I'm about to list a variety of ways families emphasize godliness in their family culture. But first a caution. Some people will surely react by saying, "We'll do them all!" "God first" is such an important core value—the core of the core—that serious believers will be tempted to go overboard.

The goal, however, is more limited: to find a way that works for your family. You'll want to choose family habits that fit the kind of people you are. They fit your lifestyle, your personalities and your interests. They fit the kind of children God gave you. They fit your schedule. You don't have to do it all. Just make sure you do *something* to build a family culture pointing toward this core value: God first! If other families point toward God a little differently, fine. We're meant to be different.

Bedtime Rituals

When children are small, many families develop elaborate bedtime rituals. These typically involve toothbrushes and pajamas, sometimes a horseback ride to the bedroom, a story, a prayer. When my children were little, these rituals could go on for a long time. Some children grow quite expert at milking them.

I invented a series of stories about Harry the Dragon. I got out my old guitar and relearned how to play so we could sing some fun songs. (My personal favorite: "Dead Skunk in the Middle of the Road.") Bedtime was the best time of the day, even though I was often so tired I started to fall asleep while saying good night. Our bedtime rituals brought a wonderful sense of family connection and comfort. I get sentimental remembering them.

Because bedtime rituals mean so much to both parents and children, they offer an excellent opportunity for the first core value: God first. You can begin with a habit as simple as putting your hand on a child as you bid good night and asking God to bless him or her. Regular benedictions may not mean much in church services, but as a bedtime prayer they definitely stick in the memories of children.

Families can get much more elaborate than that. Bedtime prayer makes powerful family culture. Some children love to pray, whether with their earliest, rote prayer ("Now I lay me down to sleep . . .") or with longer, more involved, extemporaneous prayers. As children grow older, many parents invite them to share specific concerns and pray about them together. Talking over the concerns and joys of the day leads naturally to prayer.

Quite commonly, though, children make prayer times difficult. Some refuse to pray. Others insist on "fooling around" by making joke prayers. In other words, children often resist the habit of "God first" involved in prayer. They may even refuse in an angry or defiant manner. (Here comes shocking news: children are susceptible to sin too!)

I'd recommend not to make too big a deal out of this resistance, but to keep on praying. If your children refuse to pray, simply pray yourself. Nobody is obliged to pray! The fact that you keep on praying should say: "In our family, at bedtime, we pray to God. You don't have to participate, but nevertheless we will continue!" Most often, resistance fades away— they are just testing you, and they don't want to be left out of a warm family ritual. Sometimes resistance may become a semi-permanent state. You have to use common sense and not make bedtime rituals into agony. You can be flexible about how long you pray, about who prays and about whether the prayer is silent or aloud. Nevertheless I would recommend that you keep praying. Your response to resistance says a lot about what you believe.

Many families read aloud at bedtime, either from the Bible or from storybooks. If you read from the Bible, I'd recommend that you use a modern version like The New Living Translation or The Message. Some parents are creative enough—or foolish enough—to make up their own stories. (I say foolish because once you start a story you are obliged to continue. I didn't find it easy, especially when I was dog-tired.) These stories, too, provide opportunities to emphasize the value of God first. Remember that adventurers in made-up stories can pray too. They can go to church. They can talk about God's care when they are in trouble or danger.

FAMILY DEVOTIONS

For many, family devotions are the preferred way to emphasize God first. The kind of family devotions varies a lot. Some families do them over breakfast, some over dinner, some before bed. Some follow the Anglican *Book of Common Prayer* through its written prayers and readings; some use a book of daily devotions; some read through the Bible, or a Bible storybook, or an inspirational book like *My Utmost for His Highest.*

I want to warn you (or comfort you) by reporting that few people find the experience of family devotions invariably delightful. Family devotions often interrupt somebody's favorite TV show or important phone call. When the dear child is yanked away from television or telephone, he or she won't be in a mood for devotion. Devotions can be kept to ten minutes or less, but even that allows enough time for at least one member of the family to complain that this is boring, or to pinch his sister, or to somehow interrupt the heavenly fellowship.

As a result of such disappointments, many families give up on family devotions and then feel guilty for it. I would almost put our family in that camp. I grew up on regular family devotions, but have very sporadically done them with my own family. We always wanted to do family devotions, we sometimes tried, but we often got too busy or too preoccupied to be consistent. Popie and I are very far from meeting our ideals for family devotions. I believe, however, that other elements in our family culture fill in what is missing in family devotions. No family can do everything. More important is to do something.

That said, family devotions certainly make a great contribution to "God first." The effort to have devotions says a lot, even when they turn out to be less than heavenly. Family devotions say that we make time for God. We do it together, as a family. Children will resist devotions just as they resist bedtime prayers, but working through the difficulties helps to reinforce the message.

Variety can help ease the strain. Ask your friends for suggestions. Have your child search the Internet or the bookstore for new devotional materials. Try different formats, different times, different books and different approaches. Look for a format that works for you.

For example, one family I know—a mother and two daughters—has a special carpet that is kept rolled up under the bed. When the time comes to pray together, they pull out the carpet, stretch it on the floor, and kneel, lie or sit on it. The "prayer rug" has become a visual symbol of family prayer.

The mother told me that her older daughter recently entered a phase of resistance to prayer times, mainly because she hated to be interrupted with friends on the phone. One evening the mother suggested to her younger daughter that they just go ahead without her older sister. "Oh, no, Mom," the younger daughter said. "If you make an exception now, pretty soon it will be every night." So they waited until the older girl got off the phone.

It helps a lot when your children take responsibility, as that younger daughter did. If children complain that devotions are boring, you can ask them to lead devotions in a way that peps them up. They may learn more from trying to accomplish that than they ever will from enduring your approach.

CHURCH ATTENDANCE

Not too long ago, church attendance on Sundays was mandatory. In a small town, non-attendance could cause a scandal. Church was as American as apple pie. Of course, that's no longer so. Church attendance now belongs to the realm of personal conviction and family culture.

This shift has a positive side. Church attendance has regained real meaning. Not everyone does it. When you show up at church, you make a statement: God matters.

The trouble is, church often is inconvenient. You may miss an important game on TV. You may be unable to play in an important soccer tournament. And after all, not every church service rewards the effort. Plenty of Sunday mornings you might as well have stayed in bed, for any good it does you. (I know, I know, we do it to honor God, not for ourselves. But that doesn't keep these questions from surfacing in young minds.)

For church attendance to communicate "God first," you have to attend when you really don't want to. If you attend church only when it suits you, your message is clear: we worship God when we find it convenient.

I'm a veteran of this issue, because we have made church attendance a major part of our "God first" family culture. I won't say we found it easy. When kids are young, the commitment burdens the parents. Getting everybody dressed and on their way is tough. Certainly, shoving clothes on children and rushing out the door doesn't cultivate a sense of reverence and peace. Sometimes you would feel better to take it easy and enjoy a relaxed morning at home.

When kids are teenagers, *they* bear the brunt of the difficulty—and they'll probably let you know it. Their social life probably involves Saturday night. Late Saturday nights usually produce limited interest in Sunday morning church.

Kids find it embarrassing to explain, when they stay overnight at a friend's house, that they have to get themselves up while others are sleeping in order to go to church. It requires effort too. They have to get up early, get dressed in the proper clothes (which they remembered to bring) and then get themselves to church without much adult assistance. That is a lot to expect from any kid.

Strict church attendance isn't for everybody. In our family, though, we take it even further. We hardly ever miss church or youth group. Skipping is simply not an option. We even go to church on vacation. When we're backpacking, we have our own brief service. Otherwise, we seek out a church for Sunday morning, wherever we are. We've done it on three continents, in small western towns and in national parks. We've done it in places where we don't speak the language. We've actually had some very enjoyable experiences, and our kids have seen a wide variety of churches. Church on vacation always seems difficult, though. It interrupts your rest and recreation.

We don't make church a moral issue. Other families aren't so regular at church, but we don't say they do wrong. Going to church is just what Staffords do. We tell our children that when they leave home and establish their own families they can choose what they do, but in our house, we go to church without fail.

Regular church attendance has produced a clear sense of identity for our family. Nobody even questions it any more. It has become a habit. Church attendance reinforces the core value "God first" because it shows that we'll always put worship above inconvenience or embarrassment.

YOUTH GROUP

I want to add that it's much easier if your church has a good youth group. We insisted that our children go to youth group and Sunday school as well as worship. That is a lot to ask, but we knew that the youth program was excellent. Our youth leaders made a huge impact on our kids!

If your church doesn't have a strong youth program, consider finding one that does. As an adult, you have lots of opportunities to augment whatever a church lacks. Your children don't. They have a very short window of opportunity during which they are likely to turn a childhood faith into a strong, independent faith. If they don't connect strongly to God while they are teenagers, they may never connect. I think their needs should take priority over yours during these crucial years.

One observation about youth groups: regular attendance is crucial. Fitting in to a group matters so much to teenagers that when they miss a few Sundays they feel estranged. If your child complains that the youth group is boring, stupid or full of cliques, the solution may be more regular attendance, not less. If they go every week, they'll get comfortable and eventually find a way to like it.

If, however, you think they have a legitimate complaint, find a way to fix the problem or get them to another youth group that they will enjoy.

If you detect an extra edge in my voice regarding this form of "family culture," it's because I think parents often fail to understand its importance for teenagers. They need to experience the body of Christ through their peers. Their family's faith isn't enough for adolescents. They have to make faith their own, and that requires a genuine connection with other believers of their own age.

The most likely time to make this developmental leap is high school. Some make it in college, and some long after college. Sadly, some never make it, and therefore never develop a well-rounded and independent faith.

You can't force Christian friendships on your kids, but you can put maximum energy into creating possibilities for them. Parents often don't. I have seen three reasons why.

1. *Parents meet their own needs in churches that don't provide for youth.* I've known many people who chose to attend small or eccentric churches that didn't offer good programs for youth. For a variety of reasons the parents liked those churches or felt a strong sense of loyalty. Their children didn't complain. Yet it was obvious that the children were not connecting with a group of peers who cared about God.

2. *Parents regard their children as exceptional—not fitting in with their youth group or not needing a youth group at all.* Kids will put up barriers,

sometimes insuperable ones. Yet sometimes parents buy into those barriers too readily. They shrug their shoulders and give up trying to get their kids to go to youth activities. They may even take a perverse pride in their children's exceptionalism! I have lived long enough that I find nothing to admire in a person's feeling above Christian fellowship, at whatever age. If someone can't connect with the people of God, they will never be able to live a robust faith.

3. *Parents emphasize family over peers.* Some families feel that youth activities pull their children too far from the orbit of family. They want the family to worship together and grow together. This position isn't wrong; it just fails to grapple with the fact that adolescents are in the process of leaving the family. They *have* to leave the family in order to grow up. Parents need to continue nurturing them but at the same time prepare them for the next stage. In terms of faith, that means helping them to connect to their peers in a meaningful way.

True, some kids make this very difficult, perhaps even impossible. All I can say is, keep trying. Adolescents change very rapidly. What doesn't connect at one stage may at another.

I am also well aware that many people live in areas that lack strong youth ministry. In a small town, for example, the odds aren't favorable for strong youth groups. I'd look for other ways for your teenagers to make Christian friends. Summer camps can provide excellent opportunities. So can summer mission trips taken with other teenagers.

The importance of Christian peers continues during the college years. That is why we encouraged our children to research Christian fellowship opportunities when they were choosing a college. Some schools have robust Christian groups with hundreds of active students. At other schools, Christian fellowship hardly exists. We consider this as important as the school's ranking with *U.S. News.*

CHRISTIAN SCHOOLS
The culture of Christian schools offers a way of putting God first. Some

families insist on Christian grade schools; others are more interested in Christian high schools; for still others, Christian colleges are indispensable. Often those who send their children to Christian schools feel very strongly about them. Some are frankly shocked to find a committed Christian family that goes to public school. (Homeschoolers often have the same attitude, and for many of the same reasons.)

You can make many good arguments for Christian schools. Writer Joe Bayly voiced the most potent one I've ever heard. Bayly said he couldn't imagine the Israelites sending their children down the road to the Philistines for an education.

Christian schools can provide a truly Christian worldview, they don't have to censor out religious content from what they teach, and the staff can openly exercise Christian love and discipline. Christian schools unquestionably offer a great deal.

Schools offer more than education. They have a unique entree to people's affections. The friendships formed, the loyalties forged, the "spirit" embraced give schools a deep emotional connection. You get attached to a school. You cheer for your school's teams, even after you are long graduated and don't know any of the players. You feel an instant bond with other alumni.

When parents choose a Christian school, they're saying that God comes first in an institution close to the heart. The education may be excellent, but another quality matters even more—the school honors God. Families that choose Christian schools want that God-honoring identity. The choice makes an impact on young minds.

Our family does not attend Christian schools. We appreciate that our country offers free schooling for all, and as a matter of family culture we feel most comfortable when we're mixing in the wider world. We get to know people who don't agree with us, and we can witness to our faith. We have encountered excellent public schools, and our kids have thrived in them. They do, it's true, get exposed to some non-Christian thinking, even from their teachers. We try to balance that out with discussions at home. We think they are better prepared to live in a world that is unfriendly to their faith.

I feel no hesitance at all in choosing public schools. I know it suits us. At the same time, I recognize that Christian schools make a strong statement of "God first." Our family doesn't make the statement that way. We have other ways to reinforce our core values. But I honor those who say "God first" through their choice of Christian schools. We don't all have to be the same.

CHRISTIAN SUMMER CAMPS

One of my friends is a single parent who shares custody of her children. Since her ex-husband has little interest in church, my friend would find it hard to make church attendance or Christian schools her primary "God first" statements. Summer church camps have made a crucial difference. Her children go every summer—so does she—and that time allows them a deep involvement with people of faith. Her children have become best friends with other kids from camp because they spend that time together each summer.

Setting aside a week or more of every summer for Christian camps allows parents to make an identity statement for the family. Putting God first in your vacation plans speaks volumes to children.

Christian camps also make wonderful employment possibilities as your kids reach college age. They won't earn huge sums, but "God first" will be underlined.

CHRISTIAN MUSIC

Just as with Christian schools, you can make many arguments for Christian music. Popular music is often sleazy and raw. Its music-makers are known for immorality. Christian music tries to encourage and enlighten.

Some families listen only to Christian music—and the choice has symbolic meaning. Music is so emotionally important, so close to the heart, that families make a powerful statement when they decide to listen only to music that honors God. Not every family wants to make this stand—ours does not, for one—but those who do say loud and clear that God comes first in the music of their hearts.

OPENING YOUR HOME

Some families use their homes as mission bases. Rather than seeking refuge from the world outside, they constantly ask the world home for a meal. This kind of outreach goes beyond welcoming friends and family. Families that practice "missionary hospitality" take in troubled teenagers, homeless people, foreign students, hitchhikers—anybody who needs a place to stay and a nurturing environment. These families practice hospitality from love, but also with a constant hope that they will be able to introduce—or reintroduce—Jesus to someone in need.

Families who practice hospitality are usually openhearted, people-loving and unflappable. They need those qualities because they find their lives frequently disrupted. Opening your home is hard, and it's definitely not for everybody.

"Missionary hospitality" must be a whole-family commitment. If one or two family members invite in strangers without the rest of the family's enthusiastic agreement, the rest of the family will probably resent it. Hospitality must involve everybody. "This is the kind of family we are—we invite people in."

Home is so close to our hearts that when a family consistently uses it as a place of ministry, they are saying that God's missionary Spirit is at the heart of who they are. Children raised in such an environment will never be in doubt about their family's commitment: God first.

THE TITHE

Tithing traces its roots to Old Testament practices that created a "family culture" for Israel. Every Israelite brought a tenth of the harvest to the temple, thus putting God first with the very substance of their lives. Jesus himself endorsed the practice (Matthew 23:23), and it has been followed by Christians ever since, though with adaptations to modern times. (In the Old Testament you brought your produce as a sacrifice to support the work of God. Now we bring cash.)

Growing up, I was taught to tithe my allowance: to put 10 percent in the Sunday school collection plate. I got twenty-five cents a week, and I spent considerable time every week calculating the mix of candy bars and comic books I would purchase. (Comic books were ten cents, and candy bars a nickel. I remember debating the trade-offs in my mind.) Tithing was costly to me. It meant that I could not regularly purchase two comic books and a candy bar with my allowance. I felt that as a real sacrifice. I am sure it would never have occurred to me to tithe on my own. I did it because it was a family expectation. We all had to tithe, like it or not.

I never could make out just what 10 percent of a quarter was, but in general I believe I tried—sometimes grudgingly—to do what I was supposed to do. I got a sense from my parents that tithing, while difficult, touched on the core of our identity. Tithing my own money made a profound impression on me as something solemn and deep—a feeling like what I imagine accompanied Old Testament sacrifices. As I got older I gained a sense of pride and purpose in tithing. I think this early practice taught me a lifelong habit of giving.

One family I know has four little boys. Each one has three labeled baby food jars, which they get out of the drawer every Saturday for the distribution of allowance. They each get one dollar, presented as ten dimes. Five dimes go in the "spending" jar, three go in "saving" and two go in "tithing." Every few weeks they empty their "tithing" jar into a church envelope and take it to church. This is an approach well suited to little boys. There can be few satisfactions so deep as the clink of money in glass jars.

Another family I know teaches tithing within the wider orbit of personal finance. The parents require a personal budget of each child. The children have to write a plan for what their money will go toward: snacks, entertainment, clothing, savings, tithing and so on. Allowances get distributed only when a child can account for all the money spent on the last allowance—including the tithe.

Tithing is a powerful way to practice "God first" because it applies to something tangible that children care about. Faith is therefore not an abstract and purely emotional thing. The fact that tithing applies to something as small as a weekly allowance makes an important part of the lesson. The amount of money isn't at issue. What matters is the "God first" principle. With everything we have, whether a little or a lot, we honor God first. God comes before my desire for a candy bar.

Of course, you can't expect your children to tithe if you don't do it yourself. When you freely take 10 percent off the top and hand it over to God, no strings attached, that says a lot about trusting him. What means more to people than money?

To make your tithe meaningful to your children, though, you have to do something uncomfortable: you have to talk about it. Many Christians adhere to the belief that money is a very private matter—more private than sex—and they don't tell their children anything about family finances. The children have no idea how much their parents give to the church or anywhere else.

But don't family finances affect the whole family? If giving affects everybody, then it makes sense for everybody to know about it. The whole family can discuss together what ministries or organizations to support with the family tithe. In our family we try to do this once a year, reporting on what we've been giving as a family, and taking suggestions. Thus the children as well as the parents can own the practice of "God first" with the family money. I find that my children take considerable interest in the discussion, and they sometimes come up with very good suggestions for where we ought to give. I think they are learning the joy of giving in the process.

SAYING GRACE

Pausing to thank God for food is a small token of gratefulness. Often enough the prayer gets rattled off so fast that any meaning gets lost. Taking the effort, though, day after day, does say something about God's place in your lives. When you're hungry, when you're in a hurry, even when you don't feel like it, you thank God for the food.

Some families sing their grace. My sister Elizabeth's family, which is quite musical, uses a variety of grace-songs to celebrate God's gift of food. Another family I know prays at the end of the meal, when they're not in quite so big a hurry.

The statement of "grace" grows stronger when you say a prayer in embarrassing situations. For example, when you have guests who aren't Christians. Or when you're dining in a restaurant. Kids often feel intensely sensitive to feeling "different" in such situations. (So do adults.) Learning to accept "differentness" can help them come to terms with the cost of putting God first. After all, you're rarely embarrassing or troubling other people. The vast majority of people are appreciative and respectful of prayer, even if they don't share your faith. You may be embarrassed; they are not.

Scripture certainly doesn't require that you pray before meals. Not every family will find that this practice suits them. Families who do, however, plant a memory that sticks.

BAPTISM DAYS

Whereas tithing and prayer before meals have a long history, our family invented baptism day celebrations for ourselves. I noticed that one of the key Christian sacraments seemed increasingly invisible. Even Baptist churches seemed to treat baptism as a ritual you get through and then forget. Yet baptism represents an important moment in anyone's life, when God puts his claim on him or her.

So we did a little research, found out the dates of our baptisms and put them all on the calendar. We try to recognize each baptism day. We have a special treat for dessert, talk about our memories of the ceremony and discuss briefly what baptism means in that person's life. We affirm the spiritual growth we see. Baptism day is like a birthday celebration, only without the presents. It provides just one more way to recognize God's claim to first place in our lives.

PAYING THE PRICE OF COMMITMENT

I've given only a partial list of ways to proclaim "God first!" Other practices, large and small, could be added. Some families take up a regular ministry—singing in a church musical group or cleaning the church building once a week. Some put fish symbols on their cars or cross-stitched verses on their walls.

The common qualities are consistency and cost. To show that God is first, you must do it all the time, not just at your convenience. And whatever you do must cost you. If there's no resistance, no difficulty, then "first" doesn't mean much. God comes first, which means that other desirable choices must be put down to second. The second command in the Ten Commandments—no idols—follows from the first. "God first" means putting away something you're tempted to worship.

I want to emphasize, however, that the choices belong to you and to your family. Nobody else can decide for you what price you ought to pay. If you feel obliged to try the full list of "family culture" options, or to match the faith of some other family, you may be responding to some imperative other than "God first." Perhaps you are more concerned about your image.

"God first" is not optional. God's priority is a core value for every Christian family. It should be expressed in freedom, however. Paul wrote to the Colossians, "Do not let anyone judge you by what you eat or drink, or with regard to a religious festival, a New Moon celebration or a Sabbath day. These are a shadow of the things that were to come; the reality, however, is found in Christ" (2:16-17).

Family culture is a matter of freedom—freedom to express our devotion to God in a way that suits us as people. We are not to judge each other in these matters.

FALLING SHORT

I don't know any subject more likely to bring on guilt feelings than "God first." Our relationship to God is terribly important, but invariably we fall short. "What a wretched man I am!" the apostle Paul wrote. "Who will rescue me from this body of death?" (Romans 7:24).

We each have our own failings, which weigh heavily on the conscience. Perhaps, though, we feel our children's lack of faith more deeply than our own.

I'm thinking of a family whose three daughters, now college age, have no connection with Christianity at all, even though their parents are dedicated believers. The parents assumed that their girls would naturally embrace faith. Because they were so confident, the parents left church and youth group and all other expressions of "God first" as optional. They worked harder at getting their girls to volleyball tournaments than to Sunday school. Two of the girls play college-level volleyball now, but none of the three is an active Christian. You can imagine that the parents, proudly attending volleyball games, feel some powerful regrets mixed in with their pride.

I mention this family for two reasons. One is to illustrate the importance of putting God first in your family culture. Thinking good thoughts about God and making good speeches about God won't affect your family nearly as much as some simple family rituals, like those I've listed.

Second, I want to remind those who feel like failures that they are not finally responsible for their children's faith. God is, and their children are. My friends probably did fail their daughters in certain ways, but they also gave their daughters many gifts. Thanks to their witness, their daughters know who God is and where to find him. And their daughters' lives are far from over. God is not done with them yet!

What should my friends do? They are too late to get their daughters to youth group. They are too late for regular family devotions, too late for most of the practices that I have mentioned in this chapter. They are not, however, too late to pray. They are not too late to themselves draw closer to God and let their lives serve as a living witness to the priority of God. They are not too late to rethink how they communicate their faith to their daughters. (Perhaps they have been too heavy-handed; perhaps they have been too lax.)

When we fall short, do you think it surprises God? And has it yet stopped him? "He who did not spare his own Son, but gave him up for us all—how will he not also, along with him, graciously give us all things?" (Romans 8:32). Not only is God in the redemption business, he is very successful at it. Knowing him, we should never lose hope for either ourselves or our loved ones.

4

CONCERN FOR OTHERS

Reaching Out to the Unlovely

"Love your neighbor as yourself." MATTHEW 22:39

"Love your enemies and pray for those who persecute you."
MATTHEW 5:44

*"The entire law is summed up in a single command:
'Love your neighbor as yourself.' "* GALATIANS 5:14

"Go and make disciples of all nations." MATTHEW 28:19

"Do not forget to do good and to share with others." HEBREWS 13:16

*"Seek justice, encourage the oppressed.
Defend the cause of the fatherless."* ISAIAH 1:17

*"Do not forget to entertain strangers, for by so doing some people
have entertained angels without knowing it."* HEBREWS 13:2

"Give generously . . . and do so without a grudging heart."
DEUTERONOMY 15:10

In *The Long Winter,* a book in the Little House on the Prairie series, a blizzard sets in to the South Dakota prairie during the autumn months. Giant snowdrifts completely block the train line, cutting off food and coal from the outside world. By mid-winter the town has run entirely out of food, and starvation threatens. Nineteen-year-old Almanzo Wilder and his friend Cap Garland decide to do something to save the town. They set off with two horses and a sled to try to find grain. A rumor says a lone homesteader got in a crop and stored it. If they can find him, they can save their neighbors (and themselves) from starvation.

The two young men have no map, no direction, only hope to guide them across the glittering banks of trackless snow. To keep from freezing in the sub-zero weather they run beside the sled. The winter day is short, and they have limited time. They can go only so far into the vast prairie, and then they must double back so they can make town before dark descends or another blizzard hits.

Just when they have reached their limit and are running out of time, they see a smudge of smoke coming from a snowbank. Following the smoke, Cap and Almanzo locate a homesteader, living in a sod house completely buried in the snow. He's happy to see them, since he hasn't had company since October. And yes, he has grain. But he's not going to sell. He has saved it all for seed.

"There's women and children that haven't had a square meal since before Christmas," Almanzo says to him. "They've got to get something to eat or they'll starve to death before spring."

"That's not my lookout," says Mr. Anderson. "Nobody's responsible for other folks that haven't got enough forethought to take care of themselves."

He's adamant against selling his wheat until they offer him an unthinkable price. It's a near thing—he's stubbornly not interested in selling—but Almanzo and Cap finally convince Mr. Anderson that he'll gain by selling. They load the grain and race back, almost missing the town in the dark and an oncoming blizzard. Thanks to their risky venture, the town survives.

The story stands out in the Little House books because Anderson's attitude is so unlike the normal warm neighborliness of the frontier. Let a town starve to death because you had other plans for your grain? Yet neither Almanzo nor Cap seems shocked by Anderson's selfishness. Yes, they seem to agree, life *is* every man for himself. Their only answer to Anderson's selfishness is a higher price. They must make the deal worth his while.

The story reveals another side to the American frontier. Liberty means you don't owe a thing to your fellow creatures. That shows in Mr. Anderson's claim that "nobody's responsible for other folks."

Shocking as this attitude seems next to the idealized neighborliness of the Little House books, it portrays America realistically, then and now. Today, just as in the Little House series, we stand in favor of community and kindness. Everybody admires generous, good neighbors. In the shadows lurks another point of view, however: If I choose to be kind, it's because I *choose*. If I don't choose to care for my neighbors, that's my business. I don't owe them anything.

Of all fourteen core values, the commandment to love your neighbor probably runs closest to American culture. In any ordinary public school you're likely to find an emphasis on peacemaking on the playground, canned food drives for the homeless shelter and reading-group stories stressing love for the "different" kid. Helping the needy is a driving force behind liberal politics, and not accidentally conservatives have attached "compassionate" to their label. Compassion is widely admired.

You find resources in support of compassion everywhere. Your family can make an annual tradition out of running the Human Race for charity. You can raise a puppy for Canine Companions, give canned goods to a food pantry or walk your neighborhood for the annual leukemia drive. Nobody will look at you funny or think you are overly religious.

America, with its unusual emphasis on volunteerism and charity, helps families to form a culture of concern for others. You really don't have to become too different from your neighbors.

The Bible pushes you to go further than American voluntarism, however. You're not told to love at your convenience. The command is not to care for people who are friendly and appreciative, but to love your *enemy*. You're told to turn the other cheek to someone who strikes you, and to love your neighbor with the same attention and persistence that you lavish on yourself. Such extreme loving is not part of the American way. It probably has never been part of any national culture. The Bible says (contrary to Mr. Anderson) that you *are* responsible for other folks.

Throughout the New Testament we meet people astonished by these demands. A religious leader, told to love his neighbor as himself, asks skeptically, "Who is my neighbor?" (Luke 10:29). In other words, *How far do you want to carry this, Jesus?* Peter asks Jesus how many times he has to forgive his brother. He must be amazed to hear Jesus tell him that seven times is not enough—try seventy-seven (Matthew 18:22). The disciples, though they hear the Sermon on the Mount from Jesus' own lips, are ready to kill their enemies, not to turn the other cheek (Matthew 26:52).

After Jesus' resurrection, God's Spirit has to drag those same disciples out of Jerusalem to start sharing their good news with non-Jews. They naturally tend to spread the word to people who share their basic point of view—and to leave the rest of the world out.

No one should be surprised, then, to learn that for vast stretches of Christian history people took no interest at all in sharing with other cultures outside Europe. After the revival of faith represented by the Reformation, for example, Protestants took several centuries to begin sending out missionaries. They dismissed the rest of the world from their minds.

So do most of us today. We manage to put out of our minds people all around the world—and even in our hometowns—who live in desperately needy conditions.

Nobody finds loving his neighbor easy, but caring for the enemy and the stranger takes you to another dimension. People admire that level of concern—Mother Teresa is universally admired—but they consider it extraordinary, not normal. How, then, do you create a family culture that cultivates sacrificial loving? How do you make it normal in your house?

THE TWO GREATEST VALUES

When somebody asked Jesus to name the greatest commandment, he responded with what I refer to as "God first": "Love the Lord your God with all your heart and with all your soul and with all your mind." Then he added a second command, which he said is similar to the first: "Love your neighbor as yourself" (Matthew 22:37-39). Love God, love your neighbor: they make an indivisible pair. A family that truly loves God will create a family culture that truly loves the neighbors. If you learn to love God, you will love those he loves.

Take hospitality, for example. In the last chapter I described the kind of family that routinely takes in the needy and always has some troubled teenager or down-on-his-luck adult sleeping on the fold-out bed. If you're raised in that kind of family, you get used to living by God's Spirit. As you flex with ever-changing situations, you learn to trust him. You also change in the way you see struggling people. They don't seem so frightening or strange. They seem more ordinary—like neighbors and family, people whom you naturally look out for.

Tithing works the same way. When the whole family gets involved in charitable giving, you get used to putting God before financial security. You also get in the habit of thinking about the poor and the lost. Your world expands to include people and places that most people think of as far, far away.

In this chapter I will focus on love for the alien and the stranger. All around us there are opportunities to show concern for others, so I won't concentrate on garden-variety charity. Family culture can take you beyond, to those who are different from you, far from you or scary to you.

Volunteer Where You're Uncomfortable

Serve at a soup kitchen, a mental health facility or a nursing home. You're sure to encounter people outside your normal orbit—and to change your attitude toward them.

Seen from your car, the homeless can look as scary as space aliens, slouching down a street with a grocery store cart piled with possessions. Seen up close, though, taking a plate from a cafeteria line with a toothless "God bless you," they appear much more like normal human beings—which they are. You get over your discomfort if you volunteer regularly.

I could say the same for the elderly in nursing homes. If your only contact is wild jabber and vacant stares as you walk past in the hallway, nursing home residents will likely make you nervous. With regular interaction, though, you learn that this woman was vice president at an insurance company and that woman taught third grade for twenty-five years. A man who can no longer think clearly will respond to your greeting and handshake with a huge smile. You lose your fear.

I remember one old, grumpy man in a nursing home where I visited. Al wasn't very friendly when I first met him. He seemed impenetrable and grim. Al had spent his lifetime as a professional gardener. He loved plants. People, he wasn't so fond of.

Lining his windowsill was a row of potted geraniums. When I asked about them, Al shrugged in hopeless disgust. Only gradually did I learn to understand his attitude. He longed passionately to dig in a garden again, but potted geraniums were all he could manage. He wanted a shovel and a patch of dirt—simple things. But he couldn't have them. The geraniums stood for his great love and also for his frustration. He felt that his life was over.

As I came to know what Al was going through, I began to feel compassion. For me, that grumpy, unpleasant man became a human being.

When my daughter Katie was sixteen, she spent much of a summer in Costa Rica. She lived with a Costa Rican family, and every day she took a long bus ride to help in a poor village school. The entire experience was outside Katie's comfort zone—the loneliness, the poverty, the language, even the bus ride. She felt frightened much of the time. That summer changed her. By nature shy and cautious, she took daily risks and grew into someone who loves to cross cultural boundaries.

You may hesitate to put your children in scary places. The institutions themselves—nursing homes, soup kitchens—sometimes discourage the presence of children. At the least, though, you can go to frightening places yourself and bring stories home. What you do becomes part of your family's culture too. Your children will likely follow you in volunteering when they get old enough, because they've watched you.

Over holidays, especially at Thanksgiving and Christmas, many soup kitchens welcome all the help they can get, even with the inconvenience of younger kids tagging along. Some families build a tradition of helping at the soup kitchen on Thanksgiving morning, then having their own meal at home later on.

Other families have a tradition of visiting nursing homes during holidays. Children can show off their Halloween costumes, sing Christmas carols or give out hand-made cards. If they do so on a yearly basis, nursing home visits become part of the holiday celebration. The meaning of the season becomes associated with helping those in need.

HOLIDAY MEALS

Some families always invite someone to their holiday meal—someone who is old and alone, an international student or worker, somebody they met at church or at work who has trouble fitting in to society. (Sometimes they even invite a difficult relative.) The family makes welcoming strangers a holiday tradition. Long before the holiday, they're keeping an eye open for someone to invite. That alertness helps them to reach out across barriers.

The first time you invite somebody strange to celebrate a holiday with your family, you'll feel uncomfortable. Families who do it often, though, come to feel that welcoming strangers is a normal part of family time. They wouldn't know how to celebrate the day without setting an extra place. The relationships they form open up all kinds of opportunities for service.

MISSION TRIPS

Many churches and service organizations organize mission trips to Mexico or other fascinating places. They build houses, assist in a medical clinic or teach Vacation Bible School. Some families make these trips part of their annual vacation. This requires a major commitment. Money, time and discomfort are involved. All the same, families that participate in such trips usually love them.

With a little research you can find dozens of alternatives. Get your children to help in the search, using the Internet to track down options. You can decide as a family which trip to pursue. The process of preparing is part of the benefit.

Inevitably, families who go on mission trips get to know a wider world. You'll never hear them ask that perennial question, "Shouldn't we take care of the needs at home first?" For them, the world becomes home.

Somebody may point out to you that you're not necessarily doing great good on these short mission trips. Outsiders who come in for a week or even six months can't change the system that leads to poverty, disease and malnutrition. They may witness to their faith, but unless a strong local church backs up their efforts, the fruit probably won't last. Long-term results depend more on local people or long-term missionaries.

You may feel humbled when you realize you can't accomplish much on a mission trip. Even that humbling has benefits, though. The world needs humble people—not more people who assume that they know all the answers.

INTERNATIONAL STUDENTS

More than ever, students come to the West from almost every country in the world. They need places to stay, and they need welcoming people who will help them to navigate the local scene. Schools and sponsoring organizations constantly look for families to help. They give you a great opportunity to bring the world into your home. Some families make a regular practice of taking in international students, and as a result they have a network of friends and acquaintances all over the world.

These overseas students don't usually come from economically impoverished families. But concern for others—the love of neighbor that Jesus spoke of—embraces much more than physical need. Concern for others involves spiritual concerns as well. A host family gets wonderful opportunities to reach out to students' spiritual and emotional needs. Many internationals come from quite unfamiliar religious and cultural backgrounds.

MISSIONARY FRIEND

You can become a tremendous help to missionaries by befriending them from a distance. Most churches don't have anybody doing it. They contact their missionaries by writing checks. Yet missionaries need the warmth of friendship just as much as they need checks.

The whole family can take on the job. You can put the missionary's picture on your refrigerator, remember him or her in your family prayers, send gifts at holidays and host the missionary when he or she visits your area. The responsibility of writing a weekly letter or e-mail can rotate through your family.

I guarantee your effort will be appreciated. Missionaries—and their families—often work in remote and difficult cultures. They cherish the knowledge that somebody at home remembers them and thinks about them. They appreciate letters or e-mails. At times of spiritual struggle, missionaries love to know that somebody prays for them. Missionaries often feel increasingly remote from their home. They can't relate to Western affluence because they live in such a different world. They like to feel a close personal link with somebody who is a "regular person," not a pastor or fellow missionary. Regular contact helps them to feel less alienated from their home country.

I grew up in a home where missionaries were friends and frequent guests. That expanded my world so that going to Africa myself seemed natural—scary, but natural. When Popie and I worked in Kenya as missionaries, we experienced those kinds of friendly gestures from the other side. One couple in Michigan made a point of writing regularly. We didn't know Ed and Ann well when we went, but they took us on as a project. After months and years of cheerful, regular letters from them, we felt that hardly anyone meant more to us.

If your family takes on such a role, a far-off place will become much nearer. The missionary's work—helping far-off strangers—won't seem strange or impossibly heroic. The world won't seem so vast and threatening.

"ADOPT" A CHILD

Several organizations have programs for "adopting" a child from somewhere far off. The organization you choose gives a you a picture of the child, assists you in communicating with the child and makes sure that your regular monthly gifts get used wisely. If you have the opportunity to visit the country where "your" child lives, you can meet.

For most people, the relationship never gets closer than the picture on the refrigerator. Limited as that is, it makes a good beginning. If you see a child's picture daily and give regularly to help him or her, poor children in far-off places become personal and real.

LETTERS FOR JUSTICE

Organizations that promote justice and fight for human rights rely on letter writers to put pressure on key government officials. They might request that you write to your congressman regarding a pastor imprisoned in China, or they might ask you to write to the president of Zimbabwe regarding a journalist he has imprisoned for criticizing his government.

You can easily make this part of your family culture. Family members can take turns sorting out the requests and bringing them to a family meeting. You can then decide together how to respond. One option is for each family member to address a hand-written note. You can write while sitting together around a table and send the notes off together. Writing those notes is a concrete reminder that people suffer unimaginably in other parts of the world.

FOSTER CARE AND ADOPTION

I've known several families who make a family tradition of taking in foster children. This is a major and sometimes soul-searing commitment. The foster children may have suffered abuse. They may bring deep personal problems into your home. Medical and developmental issues come up too.

Yet this act—taking in a stranger as your own child—sets the highest standard of love. Unforgettable bonds can be built. In addition, most foster families learn their way through the social welfare system, through the problems of broken and needy families, and sometimes even make connections with the foster children's original families and neighborhoods. Through involvement with a child they gain an education in a wider world of need.

Adopting a needy child can have many of the same dynamics. People adopt for all kinds of reasons—some simply because they want children of their own. Some families, however, adopt extra children even after they have their own kids by birth. They adopt to save helpless kids from a bad situation and to give them a home. Several of my friends have done this, sometimes at great personal cost. Their kids-by-birth certainly know the family's priorities! So do their adopted children.

PAYING THE PRICE

Every Christian family wants to express concern for others. But quite honestly, most busy people don't do much about it. They like to think of themselves as caring people, but they rarely reach outside their comfort zone.

Talk is cheap. So are sentimental feelings. Family culture is not. When a family makes concern for others part of their life habits, the impact can go very deep. Clearly nobody has time to do everything. We really *are* busy. Just one habitual practice, however, lived out year by year, will open a family to a wider world.

We remember birthdays, most of us. (At least we feel embarrassed if we forget.) We even send cards to relatives we don't particularly like. When our children get invited to birthday parties, we provide them with gifts even for children who aren't particularly special friends. Habits like these are built into our culture. We carry them on without thinking, because such habits strengthen ties of family and community.

Those cultural habits are good, but they mainly benefit people like us. What if we took on family practices to remember those outside our family, outside our neighborhood, outside our comfort zone? Then we would better reflect the values that, according to Jesus, matter most. He told us to love even our enemies.

Readers of the Little House on the Prairie books never learn much about Mr. Anderson, the homesteader who didn't want to sell his wheat to starving people. I feel certain, though, that he didn't grow up in a family that had a habit of feeding strangers, standing up for the persecuted, taking in orphans or helping out people whom the family found strange and difficult. If Mr. Anderson had grown up in a family with those habits, he would have been overjoyed to learn that he could save a town from starvation just by selling his wheat.

An opportunity like that may someday greet your children when they're grown. Is your family culture preparing them for the best response?

5

HARD WORK

Encouraging Willing Workers

"Six days you shall labor." EXODUS 20:9

"If a man will not work, he shall not eat." 2 THESSALONIANS 3:10

"A little sleep, a little slumber,
a little folding of the hands to rest—
and poverty will come on you like a bandit
and scarcity like an armed man." PROVERBS 24:33-34

"Whatever you do, work at it with all your heart,
as working for the Lord." COLOSSIANS 3:23

Many parents, myself included, grow enthusiastic when they consider the core value of work. For some reason we are drawn to this value more readily than others. We want our children to know how to work! We hate the thought that they might grow up slothful. In fact, when our children act lazy we get downright self-righteous. "Your room is a pigsty! Don't think you're going to that football game unless you finish your homework! And pick up those socks—do you think I'm you're slave?"

It doesn't follow, however, that we succeed in imparting the value of hard work. Parents can storm all they want, but some children tune them out very effectively. How do you get through? Building a family culture of hard work is more likely to succeed than nagging.

Ideally, you want to pass on an attitude. I know some hard workers who complain constantly about their jobs. They hate work and can't wait to quit. They only work because they have to.

Hard work with a bad attitude is better than laziness, I suppose. You won't starve. However, God wants something more and better. Paul urged the Colossians to work with their whole heart, as though they worked for God himself.

Some people find the idea of working for God unpleasant and guilt-inspiring. They believe that God watches them like a hawk, ready to pounce if they go wrong.

Paul's real intent is encouragement, however. If an athlete practices harder when the coach watches, if a singer concentrates more for a concert before the president, then Christians will always get extra energy from the knowledge that God observes their work. God is not harsh and tyrannical, but generous. ("Why do you worry? . . . All these things will be given to you" [Matthew 6:28, 33]). He is a loving Father who takes pleasure in his children's performance. Of course we want to please him.

GOD THE WORKER
Furthermore, God works with us. "My Father is always at his work to this very day," Jesus said, "and I, too, am working" (John 5:17). The Bible doesn't describe God as supervising from a distance. He has always been a working God. Think of the Big Bang in which, scientists say, unimaginable energy hurled a universe into existence. Consider the creation of life, in its unfathomable complexity. God was at work in all that. And God did not stop at creation. God continues working on our planet, right to this moment.

He pushes the sun over the horizon every morning, with new delight in its splendid light. He oversees the clover's photosynthesis, and he sends his bees into the fields for harvest. He also works with humanity, communicating with millions of his followers every day. He superintends each prayer, each conversation, each sigh. God is eternally busy, not merely sustaining the universe but transforming it.

When we work, we work alongside this fabulous, caring and creative God. However menial the tasks we do, however dull, they deserve our whole heart because God's work depends on our work.

Maybe the best analogy is wartime. When Pearl Harbor brought the United States into World War II, the whole nation changed dramatically. The Army drafted hundreds of thousands of men, automobile factories were transformed to manufacture tanks, and previously worthless scrap metal became precious. Of course, many factory workers carried on at their same jobs. They got up at the same time, worked the same shift and screwed on bolts just as before. Yet in their hearts everything about their work had changed. They knew that the front-line soldiers depended on what they produced. The future of the world depended, in part, on the hard work they did on the factory assembly line.

So it is with our work. We may not be able to trace the connections very precisely, but all good work is God's work. In whatever we do, we work alongside God and for his purposes. Knowing how he works, how can we fail to give all our energy? We try to do the work in a way that pleases him.

I grant you that an eleven-year-old boy finds it hard to see the connection between mowing the lawn and God's purposes. For that matter, a fifty-two-year-old man finds it hard.

An eleven-year-old can learn, however, the inner integrity of work. When he has sweated at something and stands before a finished job, he discovers a deep sense of satisfaction. When he has struggled with a job long and hard, and kept a spirit of good cheer even in setbacks, he experiences the pleasure of good work. This satisfaction I take as a sign of God's blessing on good work. Our inner beings respond to the knowledge that we have done something well and it is pleasing in the sight of God. Even those who do not know God show some awareness of his will when they get pleasure out of hard work well done.

Work is not punishment. The story of Adam and Eve tells how God gave the partners work to do while they were still in the garden. True enough, we experience work as frustrating and tedious, since we work in a fallen world. Yet in spite of that adversity, or through it, work pulls us toward personal fulfillment. God knows we were designed to work. His ideal for his creatures is not a perpetual vacation on a beach but a job that challenges our abilities and our strength.

Work is a foundation for the other thirteen core values. Putting God first, for example, takes a good work ethic. No one can worship well without persisting when he feels bored or tired, focusing in spite of distractions and keeping a cheerful outlook even in a worship service that isn't to his taste. Worship is work.

A good worshiper learns persistence, focus and cheer by practicing them while cleaning up the kitchen, studying for a class she doesn't like or putting up the hundredth practice jump shot when he's tired and hungry. We learn a good work ethic by living in a family culture that embodies it. If your family culture doesn't include a way to teach hard work, you need to plan for a change.

CHORES

In the old days, children worked because the family farm depended on them. If they didn't help plant and harvest, there wouldn't be sufficient food. In most homes today, the children's chores are much lighter. Sure, children help when they do the dishes, mow the lawn, clean their rooms and take out the garbage. But training has become the main reason for chores. Through menial jobs around the house, children learn that life is not a free ride—they have to contribute. They also learn the habits of work, which are physical as well as mental.

Parents often find it easier to do the work themselves. Kids will protest, stall, forget or just do sloppy work. They will break dishes, spill milk and leave ridges of unmowed grass on the lawn. They will lose your tools and fail to clean your paintbrushes. Nevertheless, the hassle is worth it, if they learn. Chores establish the culture of work within the family.

There must be a family where chores just get done, willingly and well, but I haven't met them yet. The families I know struggle over chores. Threats descend from on high; whining and complaint rise from the oppressed masses. This should be no surprise. Work is hard. Chores are the first place for many children to learn how to work, and the lessons can be a struggle.

I still remember vividly the soul-stretching weariness of finishing that last pot in the sink. It seemed to me, as an eleven-year-old, that I was enduring torture. Oh, for the freedom to abandon that last, burned-on pot! Through that pot, though, I learned how to finish a job. If your kids learn how to finish a job, you have given them an invaluable gift. If they don't, they are headed for lifelong problems.

Any hard learning requires teachers who are both patient and persistent. You don't learn trigonometry by having somebody yell at you. You learn by doing problems, under the supervision of a teacher who insists on disciplined effort but is also available to help you. So it is with chores. Parents should expect to give years, not weeks, before the concept of hard work becomes second nature. Children need parents who will help them get the lawn mower started, show them the spots they missed while washing the car and shrug it off when they break the china. They also need parents who will send them back for the third time to finish the job. They need parents who will endure their whining when they can't go immediately out to play. Parents have to avoid either of two extremes: losing their tempers over the lack of performance or giving up the effort as hopeless. With chores, only disciplined effort over time pays off.

Families vary a lot in how much work they expect from their children. Some families expect their kids to do their share of cleaning the house, to wash their own clothes and to weed the garden. They insist that kids complete a substantial list of Saturday chores before they are free to play.

Such expectations may not work with every family, though. You accomplish nothing by demanding chores that simply don't fit with commitments to, say, Saturday soccer. Some kids do have—usually with the connivance of their parents—a very complex and demanding schedule. Take your pick: lower the expectations for chores, or drop some activities, but don't pretend kids can do everything. That only results in unhappiness and nagging.

Success is better than failure. That means you are better off with a list of chores that get done than a list that seems proper to you but causes constant headaches. You do not want chores to make your children hate work because they associate chores with family quarrels and overbearing parents. On the other hand, chores so light that they amount to a joke don't allow much learning to take place. Finding the right balance takes experimentation and flexibility. And the balance is different in every family.

JOBS

My mother grew up in India as a missionary's kid. Her family had servants, and so my mother never worked as a child. When she came to America for college, working her way through school, she found the adjustment painful. She made up her mind that her children would never experience such a shock.

When I was about nine years old my mother took my brother and me out to the fields to pick grapes. We worked for three days in temperatures exceeding 100 degrees. Picking grapes is hard and dirty, and we were humbled to realize that the Mexican farmhands working alongside us could outpick us at least three to one. At the going piece rate, we made only a few dollars. I believe, though, that those three days helped fulfill my mother's intention. Picking grapes as a regular farm worker taught me the meaning of hard work in a way that chores could not. I was proud of working so hard, and even though I didn't make much money, I liked the connection between hard work and cash. (I made enough to buy some longed-for fishing gear.)

By the time I graduated from college I had held all kinds of menial jobs: bus boy, janitor, gardener, irrigation-pipe mover, window washer. I don't recall enjoying any of them, but I learned how to keep at a job and not cut corners, even when nobody is watching. I learned that working hard at a job is actually easier than loafing at it.

Some parents question the value of low-skill jobs, such as flipping burgers at McDonald's. I believe the key lessons of hard work can be learned very well at such places. True, a job selling hamburgers won't make a splash on your résumé. It will, though, teach you how to show up on time, behave responsibly, do your duty without shirking and get along with your coworkers. With those lessons learned, you'll do all right in the working world.

To underline the necessity of work, some families expect their children to buy their own clothes, cars, car insurance and stereo equipment. Some families insist that their kids pay college expenses. That way, kids learn early to be responsible with their work and their money.

I want to issue a caution, though. Jobs don't fit every family. A student cannot work many hours at a job while taking a demanding academic schedule and playing sports (or music, or drama, or whatever) at the same time. There just aren't enough hours in the day. Popie and I haven't expected our children to take part-time jobs, because we prefer their involvement at school and school activities. As long as they're working hard—whether for pay or not—we're satisfied.

HOME PROJECTS

In olden days on the farm, children got to see their parents as hard-working examples. Every teenager got to measure himself or herself against Dad's and Mom's capacity for work. Today, with most adults working at jobs outside the home, few children get to see their parents on the job. Home projects can make up for it.

Home projects let your children see you hard at work, whether sewing, knitting, plumbing, landscaping or remodeling. Obviously, you're better off if you actually know how to do these projects. If you don't, however, you'll find plenty of resources—books, videos, seminars—to help make up for your lack of experience. Almost anybody can learn how to do basic home projects. When your kids learn from you or along with you, they'll be farther ahead as adults with their own homes.

Kids rarely turn out lazy in homes where parents do home projects. I'm not saying that the experience is always pleasant. People can get downright irritable working at home projects. But so can people in the working world. Learning to cope with impatient coworkers is part of the learning experience.

SCHOOLWORK

Study is work, and those who take their schoolwork seriously learn the meaning of hard work just as much as those who work on construction. Granted, working with your mind requires a different kind of labor, but the habits of perseverance, timeliness and concentration are the same.

Some families consider homework the student's job, and therefore they don't expect the student to get a job. That has been our family choice. One cautionary word, though: if school is the student's work, the standards should be as strict as those that apply to any other job. In today's schools many students slide by while doing very little work. Families that want to teach the core value of work through school have to set some standards. For example, some families make a rule of no TV, telephone or video games until all homework is complete each night. I guarantee you this will draw resistance. But would any job on earth set a lower standard?

SPORTS

Can sports teach the meaning of hard work? They not only can, they do. Many children first grasp the importance of self-discipline when they see practice, concentration and high energy producing results at sports. In sports they first get to experience the respect of their teammates and coaches for their work habits.

My children all ran long distance in high school. They learned a good deal of discipline and perseverance through their training. Not every kid will learn those lessons through sports, though. I recall a boy on a soccer team I coached. He spent much of one game bent over at his position on the field, watching the ball from between his legs. We tried to get him to pursue the ball more conventionally, but he found the upside-down view more interesting. I like Tobin tremendously, and I know for a fact that he has grown up with an excellent work ethic. I guarantee, though, that he didn't gain it through sports. They just didn't interest him.

If your child isn't interested, you will have little success trying to drum up a work ethic in sports. You'll only manage to turn disinterest into active dislike. Find some other way to teach hard work, and let your child enjoy sports in a way that makes sense to him or her.

Some children, though, take sports very seriously. With them, parents can underline the value of hard work. A good work ethic requires that you get to practices on time, work hard at the skill being practiced and concentrate rather than shirking or goofing off. A good work ethic means not skipping practice in favor of a more tempting offer. Hard choices are involved. If parents intend to teach hard work through sports, they have to set guidelines and stick to them, just as any job would. Other claims—mealtimes, family vacations, schedules—may require adjustment. Children who really care about sports will understand the point of shooting a hundred free throws a day, or fielding a hundred ground balls. They can submit to a practice regimen that tests their commitment.

MUSIC

Just as with sports, music makes a great environment for learning to work. Everybody knows that you can't become a good musician without a great deal of practice.

As with sports, some people just aren't interested. If children can catch a spark of interest, though, and go far enough to experience the magic of creating real music, they'll understand the connection between work and success—not to mention pleasure. I notice that this happens far more often in homes where the parents themselves play and enjoy music.

The same could apply in many other artistic endeavors—painting, drama, dance. Artistic training is not for everybody. For some, though, it's the key to learning a work ethic.

SPECIALIZED SUMMER PROGRAMS

In order to understand hard work, you have to be exposed to high expectations. Students who get stuck in a class where everybody coasts, or athletes who play on a team of slackers, will never learn to do their best. Similarly, if your daughter gets a job at a retail store where she stands around bored all day, the experience won't help her understand hard work. You want to introduce your children to environments where they see others working hard and skillfully—an environment where they have to hustle to keep up.

Specialized summer programs can offer such an environment. Summer sports and music camps expose young people to outstanding instruction, demand disciplined practice and put them with a group of other young people who take discipline seriously. One of my sons got tremendous benefit from three weeks at a summer philosophy course for high school students. He was exposed to college-level expectations and hung out with some very smart and hard-working students. Lights went on in his head!

Outward Bound and other similar organizations offer deliberately demanding outdoors experiences. They take teenagers who never have felt pushed—never faced down fear of failure or been forced to keep going beyond the point of exhaustion. When kids succeed under challenging conditions, their self-confidence soars. Carefully organized programs, staffed with experienced leaders, can provide absolutely life-changing experiences. (Training and experience matter. An inexperienced leader can demand too much of young people and even put them into physical danger.)

Ultimate Values

Hard work is a prosaic value when you compare it to magnificent themes like putting God first or serving your neighbor with love. Most people would hardly even consider hard work a religious virtue. (I've certainly known some hard workers who won't be confused with any saint.)

All the same, you can hardly succeed in life without hard work. Procrastinators and sluggards are like a bicycle with a soft tire—they can function, but not properly, and people get weary of trying to make them go.

Besides, hard work *is* a religious virtue. God made human beings to find wholeness and satisfaction at work. We don't want to raise lazy children. Even if they were very spiritual and very kind, they would fail to live up to God's best intentions for them. No one can live up to his or her full potential for godliness and kindness without learning to work at it.

I've tried to make the point that you can learn hard work in many different endeavors. Chores and jobs are the common way to learn to work, but not the only way. Family culture comes into it. Find a way that works for your family, and work hard at it.

6
TRUTHFULNESS
Learning to Speak the Whole Truth

"You shall not give false testimony." EXODUS 20:16

"Simply let your 'Yes' be 'Yes,' and your 'No,' 'No.' "
MATTHEW 5:37

"Love does not delight in evil but rejoices with the truth."
1 CORINTHIANS 13:6

*"Each of you must put off falsehood
and speak truthfully to his neighbor."* EPHESIANS 4:25

"Stand firm then, with the belt of truth buckled around your waist."
EPHESIANS 6:14

"Let your conversation be always full of grace, seasoned with salt."
COLOSSIANS 4:6

"Without wood a fire goes out; without gossip a quarrel dies down."
PROVERBS 26:20

In her work as a marriage and family therapist, Popie meets all kinds of people. They tell her amazing stories about their lives, sometimes relating experiences that would curl your hair. After thirty years of listening to people who need her help, Popie is unshockable. Hardly anything surprises her—except, she will admit, one thing. She is sometimes surprised at the frequency with which people lie and the thoughtless way they do it.

Often, Popie says, people make up stuff when they don't even have a motive. They just say whatever pops into their minds.

Popie asks Rose, "Since your driver's license was taken away, how are you getting to work?"

"I get a ride from my brother Tony."

A month later it comes out that Rose doesn't even have a brother. Why did she invent Tony? She doesn't know. She had nothing to gain by making up a story. The words just came out of her mouth.

True, Popie works with a select group of people, and perhaps they don't represent the norm. Certainly, though, many people who consider themselves truthful think it natural to shade the truth under certain circumstances. They will lie rather than embarrass someone. They will lie when they're answering questions on a government form. They will lie when they don't like the person who is asking.

In other words, truth is situational: it depends on what telling the truth will gain or lose, and who is asking. Each person judges for himself or herself whether to tell the truth, and what version to tell.

I want to offer a very different perspective: truth is a core value, not a flexible means to an end. Truth should stand above me and my imperfect understanding. Truth should be valued more than superficial happiness, desired more than peace and sought after more than a tax refund. Truth is not optional because it provides our only link to reality. If we lose the link, we fall into a world of illusion where everybody is on the make and no statement can be taken at face value.

Yet truthfulness comes at a cost. When I think of transcendent truth, I think of Abraham Lincoln. I don't mean the stories about his honesty in returning a penny to the grocery store, though those count for something. I mean the fact that in an extraordinarily confused time, while leading a nation at war and under incredible political pressures from all sides, he grappled to know the truth. In his speeches he invited the public to grapple for the truth along with him. The contrast with today's politicians, who cannot open their mouths without first polling their audience, amazes me.

Every time I stand in the Lincoln Memorial in Washington, D.C., and read the solemn words of Lincoln's second inaugural address, I get tears in my eyes. That brief talk still seems like a miracle. By normal expectations, Lincoln's speech should have been all about congratulating his government, his army and the American people for saving democracy. After four long years of battle, Lincoln could predict for the first time that the Union would prevail. Those who came for his inauguration undoubtedly expected to hear something of his postwar plans to punish the Confederate rebels, to accommodate freed slaves and to reward Union soldiers and their families for their sacrifices.

He offered none of that. Instead, he gave a probing theological meditation on the mystery of the war. He did what no pollster would have recommended, speaking not one word of self-congratulation. War had unmasked the pretensions of both North and South, he explained. Both sides had thought to use war to further their ends, Lincoln said, but the astounding violence of war had worked in ways neither side had planned or expected or prayed for. Lincoln suggested that the war was punishment for the sin of slavery, a sin that encompassed both North and South. Both sides shared responsibility for slavery, and both shared suffering. In this joint punishment, God's strange work became visible, like a figure emerging dimly from the fog of war.

That work of God, as best he understood it, was the basis of Lincoln's postwar plans to reunify the Union: "With malice toward none, with charity for all; with firmness in the right, as God gives us to see the right, let us strive on to finish the work we are in; to bind up the nation's wounds; to care for him who shall have borne the battle, and for his widow, and his orphan—to do all which may achieve and cherish a just, and a lasting peace, among ourselves, and with all nations."

We have not seen a politician like that in 150 years. Partly thanks to Lincoln I can almost imagine a society where every word and gesture is genuine, intended to communicate in loving truth. I imagine a world in which politicians don't hide behind a wall of blather but say what they mean and mean what they say. I imagine friends who talk of deep truths, rather than putting up a mask of small talk. I see family members who will face difficulties with real candor, speaking the truth in love instead of pretending to feel no pain.

We don't live in that society or in that family. In our world, full of skeptical small talk, joking jabs, gossip and chatter, people rarely try to bring truth into their situation. They keep their distance from each other, and they keep truth to a minimum. You can listen all day and hear no penetrating truth.

TAKING INVENTORY

The book of Proverbs contains serious warnings about the power of thoughtless words to do harm. When I teach on those Scriptures, I like to encourage people to take an inventory of their conversation. One way is to carry a notebook with you for a week and take notes on every single conversation. Another method is to set a tape recorder on your kitchen table and record your dinner talk. What do you find when you listen to that tape or go back over your notebook of conversations? Most people find very little. Lots of words are spoken, but few would be missed. Most of our conversations are hugely vapid and subtly debilitating. Not that we want to talk like Socrates all the time, but couldn't truth and light break in occasionally?

Truthfulness is much more than the absence of lies. It is genuine communication of minds and hearts. Real truthfulness reflects the character of God, who is always exactly what he says he is, and who speaks painful but joyous truth—never any small talk—to our hearts. Think of Jesus: ever kind, but relentlessly truthful.

To be really truthful, we have to do more than stop lying. Really, most of the work is positive—learning how to speak the whole truth in love. However, truthfulness has to begin with a process of purification. Insincerity, lies and deception create such a hall of mirrors that truth, when someone speaks it, hardly registers.

Did you ever try to give a sincere compliment among a social set that constantly flatters each other? People don't take it seriously. They think the truth is weird. So purification, which is negative, makes the way for truthfulness, which is positive. We can't hope for full truthfulness until we recognize what is false and learn to eliminate it. By eliminating lies and gossip and blather, we can create an atmosphere where truth connects.

ZERO-TOLERANCE TRUTHFULNESS

In the family I grew up in, we all knew you got punished less for misbehavior than for lying about what you did. Steal a dollar from your mother's purse and you could still hope for mercy. Lie about what you'd done, and the penalty and wrath were worse. I think I only had my mouth washed out with soap once, but it was quite enough, thank you.

Not only that, but the threshold for lies was very low. My parents never tolerated the idea of a white lie.

They used a definition of lying that troubled me but ultimately made life simpler: *a lie is an attempt to deceive.* For example, if my sister was crying and I declared my innocence by claiming, "I didn't hit her," I got punished doubly for lying when it came out that though I hadn't hit her, I had pushed her. Or again, I might claim that I never touched my brother's missing baseball cards, but I lied by not adding that I had told my friend Robby to take them. Not a good idea, in *my* parents' home.

This definition of lying leads directly to the courtroom question, "Do you swear to tell the truth, the whole truth, and nothing but the truth?" You can "lie" while mouthing factually truthful statements—lie because you intended to lead the person astray with your truths. Especially when I reached an age of abstract thinking, becoming capable of more sophisticated deviousness and deception, this no-tolerance definition of lies eliminated elaborate mind games. The definition is far-reaching and easy to apply: are you trying to deceive? Then you are lying, no matter what words you say—or don't say.

Not every family will opt for the stringency of a zero-tolerance policy on lying. Some will prefer to flex, explain, discuss, warn and educate. After all, children don't immediately get the difference between lying and imagination. (When you say you have an invisible friend, is that a lie? No, because you don't intend to deceive.) For families that want to underline truthfulness in the strongest possible way, though, the no-tolerance policy makes the point very clear. My parents' strictness pointed me toward truthfulness, positively defined, because it showed me that the lack of truthfulness was taken very seriously.

FINANCIAL INTEGRITY

Money is a potent symbol. Many kids—and many adults—take money as the real arbiter of truth. They figure if you tell the truth when it hurts you in the pocketbook, you're serious about truthfulness. Create a family culture of absolute, inflexible financial integrity, and you're on your way to creating a family that understands the value of truthfulness.

So the clerk gives you too much change. What do you do? If you're truthful, you point it out to him.

What if you've already left the store and are driving home? All the better, for families who adopt the culture of absolute financial integrity. True, Safeway won't notice the $1.47. The children of your household certainly will, however, if you turn around, go back and return it to the store.

A culture of financial integrity also means no deception on your income tax or your insurance. It means no stretching your expense account. It means getting a building permit even if you think the tax assessor will never know that you added on a room. If you behave with absolute financial integrity, you can have the courage to insist that your family members do the same.

SWEARING

When Jesus told his disciples not to swear, he didn't mean to avoid foul language. He had in mind the practice of taking an oath— "I swear on my mother's grave"—to show that you are truly serious. Don't do that, he said.

The problem with swearing lies in the assumption that truthfulness comes in degrees. There's ordinary everyday truth, and then there's truth that I absolutely mean—truth I'm willing to swear on. Jesus insisted that all truth is absolute, with no degrees of seriousness. Let your yes be yes and your no, no, Jesus said (Matthew 5:33-37). Your words should be completely reliable all the time.

It may seem trivial when two eight-year-olds argue and one says, "Cross my heart and hope to die." Yet by correcting such trivial misbehavior, parents can make a point. Speak the whole truth all the time, and you'll rarely have to talk someone into believing you. Your character and your reputation will convince them.

GOSSIP, JABS, MEAN HUMOR

What is gossip? Not a lie, certainly, since it may be factually true and make no attempt to deceive. Webster's defines gossip as a "rumor, report, tattle, or behind-the-scenes information, especially of an intimate or personal nature." Gossip is nearly always about other people, and it offers information that isn't generally known. You can't gossip about yourself, nor can you gossip about the contents of the President's latest speech that you read in the paper. Gossip involves juicy and personal tidbits of information.

Most people think gossip is innocent, and some even believe that gossip adds an element of interest to conversation. The Bible, however, is uniformly negative about gossip. The reason has to do with the Bible's concern for truthfulness. Gossip is entertaining small talk that does nobody any good. It takes up air time. Truthfulness doesn't get a chance.

Gossip is closely akin to "unwholesome talk" (Ephesians 4:29), "foolish talk or coarse joking" (Ephesians 5:4), "meaningless talk" (1 Timothy 1:6), "malicious talk" (1 Timothy 6:4) and "ignorant talk" (1 Peter 2:15). At one end of this range is pointless small talk, just filling the air. At the other end are malicious words, subtly digging at people or stirring up envy and bad feeling. In practice, the two ends are not far apart, because gossip tends to be mean. It may pretend to pass on "prayer concerns" or to express real pity for some dreadful news, but the main reason for gossip is the frisson one gets from being in the know about somebody's troubles. Ask yourself whether you would be comfortable for the person you are speaking about to overhear what you say. If his or her presence would alter your words, you're probably gossiping.

My daughter Katie has an unusual sensitivity to gossip. Where she got such sensitivity I don't know—certainly not from me. As a teenager Katie began to challenge us. She was nice about it, but she absolutely refused to participate in a conversation that bordered on gossip. I found her reactions annoying. I thought she was super-sensitive and that we could barely even talk about other people, their needs and their concerns without her accusing us of gossip. Over a period of time, though, she alerted me and our whole family to the not-so-innocent gossiping we practiced.

Similarly, my friend John has an extreme sensitivity to humor. A lot of male humor involves jabs and mock insults. John felt real animus behind the jokes, which touched him on a sore spot. He wouldn't let us joke in peace. That annoyed me too, but over time I began to hear the jokes as John did. There really *is* hostility in much humor.

Sensitivities will vary. When you "screen" gossip or humor, you will probably disagree with others in your family. The conflict will raise awareness of the issues, however—which helps turn your attention to truthfulness. A rule of thumb applies to questionable speech patterns: If in doubt, cut it out.

COUNT YOUR BLESSINGS

Truthfulness begins with eliminating lies and other kinds of speech that undermine the truth. The greater task is positive, however. After you've eliminated lies and junk talk, you need to fill your conversation with truth.

Every Thanksgiving my mother sets out three pieces of candy corn by each place setting. They serve as a reminder of a holiday ritual: before we eat, each of us must name three reasons we are particularly thankful.

People do this a little grudgingly. Kids, in particular, often act skittish. It's not cool to be sincere, and they would skip the ritual if you let them. Because my mother insists, however, and because the day is Thanksgiving, we all reluctantly comply.

In the end we're always glad. Going around the table prompts a flurry of widely varied reasons for thanks. Oftentimes relatives and spouses express gratefulness for each other, voicing appreciation that hardly ever gets spoken. We recall crises and difficulties of the year and the ways in which they've been resolved with God's help. We express thanks for our circumstances, our homes, the nation we live in, our church and our community. One year somebody expressed thanks for hot showers, reminding us all of the vivid daily pleasure we get from the rush of hot water over our bodies.

We only do this ritual of thanks once a year, but the expressions stick in the memory. They set the tone for many other expressions of thanks-giving throughout the year.

The same effect can be accomplished in other ways or at other sea-sons. Christmas, anniversaries and family reunions offer opportunities to do a ritual of thanksgiving. In our family we use birthdays to carefully and systematically affirm each other. All the family members, and all the birthday-party guests, have to name something they like about the birth-day boy or girl.

When the kids were young, their friends' comments weren't very imaginative. "I think Silas is nice." "I like to play with Katie." As they got older, though, friends anticipated the ritual and learned to come up with more thoughtful compliments.

Some families count their blessings in prayer, making a point to care-fully thank God for all the benefits they enjoy.

Most people don't think of this as "truthfulness." Usually truthfulness is related to factuality—or to the absence of lies. However, the word *truthful* implies more. Truthfulness expresses the deepest truth about life. No truth is deeper than this: God is good. Truthful people speak the truth of that goodness. If your family masters the core value of truthful-ness, you will give thanks often.

My friend Marlene thinks of her father in this regard. He passed away this year, a surgeon who had an amazingly gentle and thankful spirit. "He might have seen very difficult situations in surgery that day," Mar-lene writes, "but he knew that, in truth, we had much for which to be thankful and he frequently expressed it. This gave all of us the bedrock assurance that God is, indeed, in control (despite difficulties) and that in the end God will win."

Marlene notes that while her mother had a very strong influence on the family's plans and finances, her father's thankful spirit controlled the family's emotions. "He bequeathed that positive emotional energy (and an attitude of trust in the Lord) to each of us children." She remembers their last Christmas together, when her father concluded a time of prayer by laying his hand on each family member and giving each a blessing. Such "thankfulness as truthfulness" left an indelible mark.

MEMORIZING SCRIPTURE

Some families learn the Bible by heart. They memorize together, every night or every morning going over passages of Scripture that they've agreed on. Alternatively, some families encourage individual memorization, by rewarding verses learned or psalms memorized. Almost every Christian learns a few verses by heart, but some families take memorization very seriously. You can learn a lot of Scripture if you work at it systematically and encourage each other.

Learning Scripture encourages you to be, literally, "truthful." God's truth becomes a part of your mind, always available for reflection and meditation. Scripture spills out into speech, and even into your behavior.

READING ALOUD

Many families read stories aloud every night to small children, and a few families continue the practice far into adulthood. Eugene Peterson, translator of The Message, has read aloud with his wife Jan for their entire married life. I may be stretching to consider this a "truthful" habit, but I don't think so. If you choose books carefully, and discuss them thoughtfully, truth will find a place in your soul.

Philosopher Kevin Vanhoozer once told me that he learned about moral philosophy while reading Dickens and Dostoyevsky on the beach in Santa Barbara. Fiction, he said, gives you a chance to test out a life—to watch from the inside as a person faces decisions and deals with difficulties, and to see whether the character's approach is one you want to adopt. Such moral reflection becomes even more possible when you read aloud, because you can think about characters and their dilemmas together.

Some of my favorite activities in raising children had to do with reading the Little House on the Prairie books, C. S. Lewis's Narnia tales and J. R. R. Tolkien's *Lord of the Rings*. Through the characters of those books we lived a life of courage (and fear), faith (and doubt), hard work (and sickness). Those books, among others, stocked our shelves with truth—truth lived out.

Movies and television offer some of the same opportunities for learning about truth, though not to the same degree or in the same way. Books are unusual in that we can stop the action, and take a moment or even a week to reflect on what is happening. A book does not need to be read in a headlong rush; the reading is enriched rather than interrupted by people's comments. (If people want to talk while I'm watching a film, they're bound to annoy me.)

Heart-to-Heart Talks

Truth confronts. If you read Scripture, you can't avoid its challenging, assertive nature. Jesus himself spoke sharply, some would say harshly, in confronting religious leaders of his day. Truth is not necessarily easy to bear.

The trick is to speak the truth in love. Sometimes truthtelling speaks so harshly that love gets overwhelmed. Sometimes children can't wait to get out of the home to escape the rasp of a father's tongue or the blunt edge of a mother's criticism. When I read memoirs of a century ago, I get the impression that that sort of truthfulness was common.

In our times, I suspect the other extreme holds sway. Many families avoid confronting unpleasant truths as long as possible. Sometimes parents lack the courage to confront. They ignore their fears, make a few half-hearted admonitions and hope for the best.

Westminster Seminary's David Powlison once remarked to me that most Christian parenting books are behaviorist in their approach. They treat children almost in the way that behavioral psychologists experiment with pigeons, controlling their behavior by carefully constructing their environment. A combination of rewards and punishments, carefully calibrated, is supposed to make all the difference.

Powlison made the point that, while rewards and punishments are appropriate, the Bible suggests a powerful role for the heart-to-heart talk of parent and child. The book of Proverbs, particularly, repeats the appeal:

- "Listen, my son." (1:8)
- "My son, do not forget my teaching." (3:1)
- "Listen, my sons, to a father's instruction." (4:1)
- "Listen, my son, accept what I say." (4:10)
- "My son, pay attention to what I say;
    listen closely to my words." (4:20)

- "My son, pay attention to my wisdom." (5:1)
- "Now then, my sons, listen to me." (5:7)
- "My son, keep your father's commands
  and do not forsake your mother's teaching." (6:20)
- "My son, keep my words and store up my commands within you."
  (7:1)
- "Now then, my sons, listen to me." (7:24)
- "Now then, my sons, listen to me." (8:32)

What the father wants his son to hear is *teaching* and *warning*. He speaks very practically about temptation and urges the son to follow truth instead of error.

If you think of it, God's chief way of influencing his people is just the same. Yes, he offers rewards and punishments. Yet the burden of Scripture is an appeal: Listen to God! Hear his eloquent plea! Turn around and come back to him before you are too late!

Popie and I have found a heart-to-heart talk our single most powerful weapon for influencing our children. Of course, we use rewards and punishments. What's more, we talk to our children all the time. We try to speak truthfully at meals, and while driving in the car, and at church. Occasionally, however, when we feel deeply troubled, we call the child privately into our bedroom. The two of us generally do this together, underlining our seriousness.

We begin with approval and affirmation, to set the context for our discussion. We might assume that our children know we love them deeply, and admire many of their qualities, but we believe we should say it, and emphasize what we say by giving detail. We tell our children why we admire and appreciate them. After that, though, we talk about our concerns. Our tone is not that of the hanging judge. Our tone is that of loving parents who would give the world to help their child. We want to communicate our anguish and our pain. We also want to communicate that the way the child is going is intolerable and that consequences are bound to come. We've had tears and trembling and all kinds of angry behavior during these conversations. They are not easy for us. They are not easy for the child. Yet sometimes these talks have had great results. Heart-to-heart talks are truthfulness full strength. They have the power to change lives.

You should surround a heart-to-heart conversation with prayer, before, during and after. Before a heart-to-heart we have often called grandparents, youth pastors and other close friends to ask for their prayers. We feel the need for God's help. That's because such a conversation aims for the heart. Only God can change the heart of a person, whether child or grownup. A parent's part is to speak the truth in love and pray for God's help through his Spirit.

AS GOOD AS YOUR WORD

Earlier eras made much of a person's word. It was a great compliment to say of people that they were as good as their word, or that a handshake was all you needed to make a binding agreement. That spirit lies behind Jesus' strong admonition against swearing. If you have to say more than yes or no, Jesus said, this comes from the evil one (Matthew 5:37).

People still admire such reliable truthfulness. Few people stress it, however, nor does anyone teach much about truthfulness in school or at church. We need a family culture of truthfulness to drive home the value.

Truthfulness has two sides. One side is purification, the elimination of lies and all kinds of talk that undercut the truth. The other side is "truth filling," which happens whenever the truth becomes deeply embedded in our minds and our lives. Family culture plays a powerful role in making truth filling a habit, regular and routine.

I can't neglect saying, however, that one kind of truthfulness is deadly. Some people are brutally truthful. Whether you want to hear their opinion or not, they tell you their understanding of the truth. Sometimes their words are devastating. They offer truth without grace.

The truth can be hard to bear. It can cut deeply. But truth as God wields it always ultimately heals and reconciles. God's truthtellers are quick to forgive and to sympathize with weakness. In God's world, truthfulness always stands close to love. And, "love is patient, love is kind. . . . It is not rude. . . . It is not easily angered, it keeps no record of wrongs. . . . It always protects, always trusts, always hopes, always perseveres" (1 Corinthians 13:4-7).

7

FAMILY UNITY AND LOVE
Holding Together in a Splitting World

"Honor your father and your mother." EXODUS 20:12

*"Unless the LORD builds the house,
its builders labor in vain."* PSALM 127:1

*"How good and pleasant it is
when brothers live together in unity!"* PSALM 133:1

*"Wives, submit. . . . Husbands, love. . . . Children, obey. . . .
Fathers, do not exasperate."* EPHESIANS 5:22, 25; 6:1, 4

*"If any woman who is a believer has widows in her family,
she should help them and not let the church be burdened with them,
so that the church can help those widows who are really in need."*
1 TIMOTHY 5:16

I recall a conversation with a Nigerian friend, Enobong. When we first met he had as little exposure to Western customs as I had to those of Africa. As we sat sharing our national traditions, it gradually dawned on Enobong how differently we saw family. I watched dismay slowly capture his face. "Do you mean to say," he stammered, "that if your brother were jobless, he would not feel free to bring his family and stay in your home? That he would need to ask your permission first?"

When I admitted it was so, Enobong dropped his eyes, as though looking into mine any longer brought unendurable pain. It seemed to be the saddest news he had ever heard.

I love my family, and I can get as sentimental about it as anyone. Living in Africa, though, showed me that my family loyalty is quite weak compared to much of the world.

Of course we Westerners love the idea of family. We talk about it fondly, nostalgically. Many of our favorite movies and TV commercials trade on family feeling. When family interferes with our lifestyle, however, we quickly put a limit on its claims. Westerners value their independence more than family, which explains why my brother would hesitate before moving his family in with mine. It also explains the prevalence of divorce. To preserve a marriage you sometimes have to put your claims on self-fulfillment on hold, at least temporarily. Westerners are not consistently willing to make that trade, not willing to tough it out in a difficult marriage for the sake of keeping the family together.

The truth is, we are conflicted. We love our families. Yet Enobong's total loyalty to family feels impossible to us.

Our world needs strong families, and we long for strong families, but they have certainly grown more difficult to form. A friend of mine, when he speaks of his family, includes not only his wife and her family of origin, but his own father (divorced and twice remarried) and his father's two subsequent wives, each of whom he refers to as his mother. Both those marriages have produced children, whom my friend counts as his siblings. In addition, he has his mother and her present lesbian partner. He includes various grandparents, cousins, and offspring relating to each of the significant fathers and mothers in his life. He likes all of them, and he happily relates to all of them as family. Yet unquestionably his loyalty to them—and theirs to him—has to be negotiated one relationship at a time. There's no fixed expectation. How could there be? It's all too fluid.

Not only do families split and recombine in new ways, they are spreading out. I have siblings coast to coast. We see each other once a year if we are lucky. Who do you call on when you face disaster? Not necessarily your brother who lives a continent away, no matter how much you love each other. One typical dilemma of modern times: an ailing, aging parent needs to go into a nursing home. Who makes arrangements and provides emotional support when the grown children are scattered in every direction and none of them lives in the same state?

Most people still want to get married and have children, and most still want to gather the extended family for an old-fashioned Thanksgiving dinner. They want traditional family life, but they find it more and more difficult to sustain. The biggest obstacles may be economic. A high proportion of mothers work outside the home and aren't available as full-time "homemakers." Few fathers come home from work at 5:00 so they can play ball with their children or watch a ballgame with their cousins. College graduates think nothing of leaving their hometowns in order to get a better job.

The modern world is not family-friendly. Its consciousness is built on the individual—individual tastes, rights, opinions and careers. Family comes in second place. Therefore families often don't hold together in love.

Since our culture does not support family very deeply, family culture must do so.

THE DARK SIDE OF FAMILIES

"Dad, why is it important for us to be close to our family?"

We had just returned from a family wedding, and my teenage son, Silas, was pondering the expense and trouble we had taken to get there. He had missed his school prom, a big track meet and a choral competition, all for the sake of an event with people he didn't know all that well. He wasn't rebelling or even complaining. (He'd done that earlier.) He was just asking, what is so important? Why do we feel obliged to skip events we are certain to enjoy for other events involving people who only share our gene pool?

I started to say that God tells us to stay close to family. Before the words got out of my mouth, though, I realized that God's directions aren't quite that absolute.

One of the Ten Commandments says, "Honor your father and your mother" (Exodus 20:12). Other Scriptures give directions on your responsibilities to family members. The Bible generally assumes that God's people should show loyalty to family. Yet Jesus told his disciples, "Anyone who loves his father or mother more than me is not worthy of me; anyone who loves his son or daughter more than me is not worthy of me" (Matthew 10:37). He wanted his disciples to know that loyalty to family might crash into loyalty to him. For a society that placed family near the pinnacle of values, that was a radical statement.

I next started to tell Silas something about happiness. Among my deepest aspirations for my children is that they fall in love, build a solid marriage, raise wonderful children and bring those grandchildren to visit me. You can be happy without family, I know, but at a deep gut level I see family as the easiest and best road.

I want my children to love their brothers and sisters. I want them to know and enjoy their cousins, aunts and uncles. In my personal memory bank are many family gatherings: Thanksgivings, Christmases, summer picnics, weddings, baptisms and anniversaries. Old photos lovingly record these events: the cousins lined up in stair-step formation, the new baby flanked by beaming relatives, the bride and groom with a full complement of grandmas, cousins, aunts and uncles. These photos grow dearer to me as I grow older. Family means stability. Family means love.

Even as I started to say this, though, I realized that family doesn't always mean happiness. It can also mean heartache, frustration and irritation. I've been blessed with a wonderful, stable family, and even for me, family is a mixture of joy and aggravation. For some people, getting close to family is like getting close to a toxic dump.

Modern individualism isn't the only obstacle to family unity and love. Real families create their own obstacles. Family gatherings can be miserable. We know; we've attended them. We have seen some nasty family fights. Families we know have a history of sexual abuse, alcoholism and other severe dysfunctions. And so families have always been.

Tough old men get weepy remembering how the family played board games around the wood stove. They forget, conveniently, that Uncle Jack was a drunk who snapped your head with his finger so hard it ached a week; that cousin Daniel went to jail for stealing Grandpa's Social Security checks.

Sometimes the closest families become the most destructive. Remember, mafia families are close—close enough to kill. Or think about Enobong. His people's unquestioned family loyalty can show its face as tribalism, which, when it turns hostile, can be the cause of violence and murder.

As I pondered my son's question, I arrived at what I believe to be the basic reason for staying close to family. Families are the raw (and I mean raw in all its senses) material for our spiritual growth. They are the environment where we most poignantly experience reconciliation and forgiveness—and where we most blatantly need it. Families bring out all our longing for love and acceptance. Then they let us experience the human flaws—in us, as well as in our relations—that keep us from it. In this crucible of hope and frustration, we can learn what it means to be redeemed.

CONFRONTING SIN IN FAMILIES

I know my reaction when I run into meanness and hurt in family life. I want to get out! I want to escape and stay clear of this family forever. To do so, however, would mean missing out on the full, healing grace of family life.

Read the book of Genesis. One family story follows another, but none of them glows with nostalgia. Rather, we read tales of lightning-slashed quarrels between relatives. To name only the best-known cases: Cain and Abel, Abraham and Lot, Sarah and Hagar, Isaac and Ishmael, Jacob and Esau, Rachel and Leah, Joseph and his brothers. These characters are jealous, selfish, competitive and mean. They put their very best and their very worst into fighting each other.

Joseph's story forms the climax of Genesis, taking more space than that of any other character, including Abraham. Yet it is a tale of hateful sibling rivalry. In bone-chilling brevity, Genesis tells how eleven brothers nearly murder their youngest sibling, an insensitive, spoiled Daddy's boy. Instead of death, they give him a break—they sell him to some passing strangers. He ends up in an Egyptian prison, forgotten.

The rest of the tale describes how the brothers work their way out of this unforgivable sin. The story is dark and convoluted, filled with false hopes, further betrayals, tears, tricks and disguises. Though God plays no visible part, Joseph is sure that he works behind the scenes. With tears Joseph tells his brothers in the end, "You intended to harm me, but God intended it for good" (Genesis 50:20).

Hardly any of us has family secrets as lethal as Joseph's. His family story would fit well in some violent gangland ghetto. Yet here is the most astonishing news: God chose Joseph's terrifying family as his pathway into the world. God plans to use these people, of all people, to redeem a broken world. His motto seems to be, "If you can save this family, you can save anybody!"

And so it happens. In the New Testament, adoption into Joseph's family gets offered to anyone who wants it. Thousands flood in, eager to experience love and forgiveness. Today we call that family "church." Whatever the name, it remains a family. Its members are addressed as brothers and sisters, fathers and mothers. They remain as imperfect as the original family in Genesis. Yet at its best, this family shows the ability to grapple with sin and to reconcile siblings.

Most people feel pain in their families. We long for closeness, but our relatives wound us, infuriate us and irritate us. And we irritate and infuriate them. Around our relatives we can act like jerks: moody, suspicious, overreacting, overemotional, cold. I'm not speaking theoretically. I have been that jerk.

More than modern trends make family difficult. Our hearts make family difficult. To strengthen the core value of family we must deal with the heart.

God is the surgeon. He transforms darkened hearts. We don't. Our job is to stay on the operating table. He operates on us within our families and through our families. Family unity and love are core values because they hold us together long enough for us to experience healing.

Here are some patterns you can work on as a family until they become helpful habits that reinforce unity and love.

MAKE YOUR SPOUSE A PRIORITY

The root of family is the marriage relationship. I notice that people often overlook this when they talk about family. They talk about parents and children, skipping over the parents' relationship. That is a mistake. The health or sickness of the marriage affects the entire family. If husband and wife fall apart, the family falls apart.

Spouses reinforce the strength of family when they put each other first, visibly and obviously. I learned one simple way from Walter Trobisch, a pastor and missionary who wrote wisely about marriage and family life. When he came home from a trip, Trobisch always went straight to his wife, Ingrid, to kiss her and greet her. If the children ran eagerly to him on his arrival, he walked past them to find Ingrid. No doubt this approach provided his children with a small shock. Trobisch intended that it should. He wanted his children to know and feel that his love for his wife came first. On that stable relationship the children could rest secure.

Second-honeymoon trips accomplish much the same objective. When husband and wife go away together, leaving children behind, they show the children that their marriage comes first.

The logistics of arranging babysitting for a weekend away are complicated. Leaving can be emotionally difficult as well, since children often dominate our time and feelings so much. Some parents find it embarrassing and difficult to explain to the children what they plan to do! Yet cutting through those difficulties makes a lasting impact on your family.

My mother often repeats the saying, "The best gift you can give your children is to love your spouse." Some families have a tradition of not getting divorced. They aren't necessarily superior people, and their marriages aren't perfect. A lot of their staying power comes from fierce dedication. They put a priority on their marriage and thus set the tone for their children's marriages. A strong marriage—which may be a difficult marriage—makes an impenetrable core for a strong, united family.

FAMILY MEALS

The evening meal is a powerful instrument of family unity. Most families say they wish they could sit down together every night, but they just

can't. Work schedules, athletic events, music lessons and church commitments all get in the way.

You can do it if you're determined. Some families make mealtimes absolute. For others, some level of compromise is possible. You can work
on your schedule so that you all eat together four times a week. Even that
requires a struggle, if you are active people. It means planning ahead,
calendars in hand, and it means saying no to some wonderful events. If
you don't work hard at it, though, meals together will soon be rare.

One family I know committed to eating together every night. They are
a very active family, and as the three kids grew older and their schedules
more complicated, sometimes the whole family could not gather until
9:00 or 10:00 at night. Nevertheless, they would wait to eat until all five
were present. After the meal they would talk about the day and pray,
concluding with holding hands and saying the Lord's Prayer. Then each
family member would offer something he or she was thankful for. Dinner concluded with three hand squeezes—I . . . LOVE . . . YOU.

You can try breakfasts as an alternative. Some families get up a half-
hour earlier in order to sit down to eat together every morning. It helps
if you cook favorite foods on a regular basis, such as waffles.

Another option: Sunday brunch. If you get only that meal together,
make the most of it. Pull out the stops and make it a grand repast.

Once you develop a plan to eat together, you have to insist, somewhat
inflexibly, that everybody make the meal. No spontaneous decisions to arrive half an hour late! And you have to turn off the TV. Yes, even when a big
game is on. You're saying, loud and clear, that family togetherness takes priority. Believe me, there is no end to big games, favorite shows and unforgettable specials. Use the VCR to record them. Turn on the telephone answering machine while you eat, and linger over the meal in conversation.

If you don't eat together very often, conversation may be a strain
when you do. Actually, any time you have children, conversation can be
a strain. When they're young, the fussing, fighting, spilling and pouting
can wear you out. When they're teenagers, strained silence or voluble
complaining may make you long for the days of inarticulate wailing.
Family togetherness is not a constant joy.

Family togetherness isn't *supposed* to be a constant joy. The warm memories come later. You are setting a foundation to build lives on. Foundations are not made of glamorous materials. Large amounts of solid, gritty stuff make foundations. Day in, day out, foundations hold houses together. Day in, day out, mealtimes bring us together.

ATTENDING EACH OTHER'S EVENTS

When parents attend their children's Little League games, ballet recitals, school plays and choir performances, they show loyalty: I *will* support you, every time, whether I am interested or not. This is not the easiest commitment to make (yes, those hours add up), but it does communicate that you care about the events your children care about.

Some families go farther, making a rule that children attend each other's events whenever possible. You'll pay for such a commitment, because children don't necessarily enjoy watching each other's activities, and they will let you know it. However, you're making a statement: As a family we support each other all the time, not just when we feel like it. You're also making an investment in sibling friendships, because children learn more about each other's worlds. Those shared memories can result in their growing closer to each other rather than farther apart because they have so little in common.

FAMILY NIGHT

You can set aside one night a week, or one night a month, as family night. A lot of families use Monday because that night is least likely to conflict with other activities. Of course, choosing the day is a family matter. So are format and goals, which can vary. The idea is to get everybody involved. Often the planning responsibility rotates through the family. I know of one family that uses no structure whatsoever except rotating leadership. One week the twelve-year-old son may lead the family to a video arcade; another week the mother may take them all to peruse a bookstore while drinking cappuccinos. Every member of the family has complete authority on his or her night. Rotating leadership communicates that everybody's point of view has value in the family, and that the

whole family will honor each individual's sense of fun. The only fundamental requirement is that they have fun together.

Other families use their night for a "family council," sharing problems, making plans or praying for each other. Some families give every
member an opportunity to present what they perceive as a family problem, with a solution to be reached by consensus. (This format won't
work if Dad or Mom uses the family council to push through an agenda.)
For example, Dad might pose the problem that tools don't get put away.
The family then brainstorms how to improve this situation.

The way you run family night is really a matter of taste. Some like the
formality of working like a committee, and some would hate it. The
point is, your family finds its own style and becomes accustomed to
working together. That creates a very different idea of family. It is no
longer just an accident of genetics, or of a shared domicile. The family
becomes a working organization, functioning in harmony.

SUMMER VACATIONS

I particularly remember "the vacation that ate the summer," as I fondly call
it. I needed to do research at various sites across the country, and we decided to make it a family trip. Our three kids were all school-age, and none
of them particularly liked to be in the car. In fact, they hated the car. As we
set out to drive across the country, Popie and I had our doubts. I told her
reassuringly that we could always turn around and come home early. I
couldn't imagine spending weeks together packed in that little minivan.

It wasn't all fun. We were stuck with each other twenty-four hours a
day, without telephone, television, friends or work. We lived through
miserable, steamy weather and long, boring drives through featureless
country. Yet a sense of togetherness grew as we fell into a rhythm of
travel. We had no choice but to get along, so we did. Our isolation from
the rest of the world helped to weld us together. We had a great time.

Vacations have a huge effect in unifying families. Any time you take
time to play together, you benefit. The best vacations involve the fewest
distractions. Letting your kids take friends along for company may make
them happier, but you probably won't get quite such good time as a fam-

ily. A packaged Disney tour can be great fun, but you might get more out of a long car trip or a week at a mountain cabin.

FAMILY CHORES

We've discussed chores in the chapter on work. They deserve mention in a chapter on family unity as well.

Many families require chores of every member: washing dishes, taking out garbage, washing cars, walking the dog and so on. You may assign chores to teach the value of work or simply because you want help. I think the best reason is that chores teach family unity.

When children do chores, they actually contribute to the family welfare. From this participation they gain some sense of ownership. The family belongs to them; they have a part to play. And this creates a stronger sense that the family is a unit, in which every member contributes.

BIRTHDAY AFFIRMATIONS

Birthdays are a great invention. The concept is simple but profound: take one day out of the year to celebrate the life of each family member. This communicates year after year that each family member is a cause for joy, not because of what they contribute but simply because they were born. Graduations and anniversaries celebrate achievement, but birthdays celebrate life. Whether you are sick or well, big or small, pretty or plain, bright or dull, you get a birthday.

Popie, a great encourager, introduced birthday affirmations as a way to underscore the point. For each birthday, we go around the table and get every family member to say at least one thing that he or she appreciates about the birthday celebrant.

Birthday affirmations level the playing field, so that Mom isn't the only one doling out compliments. Everybody has to do it, and everybody has to come up with something positive to say. Over time birthday affirmations make us all think more deeply about each other's qualities. They help us to appreciate each other more. The fact that our three children all currently like and admire each other we owe at least partly to this ongoing family ritual.

BIRTHDAY CARDS

So far I've focused on the nuclear family: Mom, Dad and kids. To experience the full, robust support of family you must include grandparents, uncles, aunts and cousins. They give a wider sense of support, and a bigger sense of identity. It's encouraging to grow up connected to an extensive family system. There is strength in numbers.

Remembering birthdays with a card or a note serves as an annual reminder of your attachment to cousins, nieces and nephews, not to say grown-up brothers and sisters. The whole family can sign the card and scribble a line—maybe even draw a picture.

To prod my memory, I have programmed my computer calendar to alert me four days before each family birthday. That gives me time to get off a card that will arrive on time. I also try to keep a batch of birthday cards on hand, ready to send. As busy as I am, and as careless about birthdays as I tend to be, any barrier to sending the card will probably stop me.

You can go further and send gifts. If you have a large extended family, though, that gets expensive. Also, you may find yourself floundering in the dark trying to buy something a thirteen-year-old boy will appreciate. All the same, the attention required—which may include a phone call to learn what kind of gift might be valued—keeps the connection alive.

Family connections are easy to maintain when you're in constant contact, or when you feel close to your relatives. Rituals fill in the blank during more difficult periods when you seem to have little in common or when you just keep forgetting each other. A birthday card may or may not be meaningful to receive, but it is *always* meaningful to send, because you have to stop and think about that relative for at least a few minutes. By remembering birthdays you keep the connection alive.

FAMILY REUNIONS

I grew up with Thanksgiving dinners bringing together over one hundred members of my extended family. From those annual events I learned how much turkey I can eat, and also who my second and third cousins are. Certainly our relationships never went too far beyond the superficial. We met just once or twice a year. Nevertheless, I knew that I had a lot of family, and that the members cared enough to come together for that day. I knew who my relatives were, and I felt comfortable with them.

Family reunions keep connections alive better than birthday cards. They bring children into the picture, letting them get acquainted with uncles and aunts and cousins. Children learn to balance out their parents' peculiarities with other family models. They see that the family characteristics can be lived in more than one way. That offers a sense of security and freedom. There's a largeness in extended family.

In our busy and mobile society, extended families find it difficult to get together. My family stretches coast to coast, and my wife's is nearly as physically dispersed. If we don't work at it, we can go years without seeing each other. That is why we stay alert to opportunities for family reunions. When vacations or business bring a number of us into the same geographical region, we try to take advantage. When important birthdays or anniversaries approach, we plan ahead so everyone has a chance to gather.

Any particular gathering may be more or less pleasurable. Sometimes I find them quite painful! Yet they do bring us into contact with each other. If we only catch a snatch of each other's ongoing stories, at least we know something. (Sometimes those fragments come together much later.) Group photos taken at these extended family reunions—and even the photos are a pain to organize—seem much more precious now than they did when we took them, years ago.

Some families organize annual picnics on Memorial Day or the Fourth of July. Some go camping together. Some rent accommodations at a resort and have co-vacations. Then cousins get to know each other in a way they generally won't at a one-day event. Family camp offers another option. Many conference grounds offer one or more weeks for the whole family. A family I know made such a camp an annual event for the extended family. They got to be together in a setting where they could see a lot or a little of each other, as they chose, and have all the meals provided. They liked singing together and hearing inspiring speakers. They liked not having to struggle over the logistics.

When you gather as extended family, you are almost bound to discover how different you are. Families are required to love each other, but not to like each other—and they often don't. Sometimes the emotions can get quite strong!

No one person can remove the strain, but my friend Marlene mentions a few tips that help. For example, somebody often arrives late to family gatherings, to the considerable inconvenience of those who have planned the event. Nevertheless, complaining won't help. Neither will shunning the offender. Instead, skip the moral reproval and make it a point to rejoice that they have arrived!

You can easily get wrapped in knots worrying about schedule and agenda, considering the different tastes and different priorities of all the people involved. Instead, Marlene says, concentrate on relationships. Don't spend too much time worrying about the "right" way to eat together: the menu, the table setting. You're bound to have different ideas on all that, and since you only do this once in a long while, why fuss? Instead, try to renew your love for the people you're with, or get better acquainted with a family member whom you've only superficially known.

COUSINS' WEEKEND, GRANDPARENTS' WEEK

One family I know has an annual event known as "cousins' weekend." All the cousins in the extended family camp out together (with one set of adults to keep them alive). The kids see it as an adventure, and they love it. The parents enjoy knowing that the cousins get to know each other fairly well.

Another approach is grandparents' week. Grandma and Grandpa invite their grandchildren to stay for a week, usually just one or two at a time. It can be a very special time for the grandchildren (and grandparents!), and it gives the parents a break. Lifelong bonds between children and grandparents can result.

Lots of other rituals are possible. My dad took each of his grandchildren for an evening in San Francisco when they turned twelve. The expectation of the event made a large part of the fun. Years in advance, the children looked forward to the San Francisco trip as one way to mark a momentous event—their twelfth birthday.

In all these family habits, you have to figure out what suits you. There isn't time to do everything. The question is, do you do anything to promote family unity and love? If you don't, the results are predictable.

SETTING BOUNDARIES

I'm sorry to say that extended family commitments can clash with loyalty to your nuclear family. Mother-in-law jokes originated in some real experiences. Real mothers exist who do everything but bite the young woman whom they find hopelessly inadequate to meet their son's needs.

Jealousy isn't limited to mothers. Any relative may undercut your family, criticizing lifestyle, character or choice of job. The core biblical text about marriage, given in Genesis 2:24 and quoted several times in the New Testament, says that a man must *leave* his father and mother and be united to his wife. Paradoxically, family begins with a decision to leave the family that raised you. Sometimes that requires a very deliberate decision to tell overbearing family members where to get off. If you live in the same town, work in the same family business or go to the same church, you're more likely to need to set clear boundaries. For example, some people have to privately ask family members to keep their opinions to themselves. In the extreme, they may have to cut short relations with those who keep butting in.

Sometimes extended families do damage through their good intentions. They may smother you with a constant schedule of family activities and celebrations. How could you miss your niece Julie's birthday party? Everybody in the family was there except for you!

Young families need time and space to find their own way, and too much extended family can make that impossible. A woman may really feel that it's a crime to miss Julie's birthday, while her husband feels that one more birthday party will make him vomit. A husband and wife can very easily feel their love for each other tested against their loyalty to extended family.

When these tensions arise, husband and wife need to draw together.

You need to consciously see your spouse's discomfort as *your* discomfort, so you can strategize together about how to make it better. For example, you can set a maximum of one extended-family event a month. If one of you feels isolated and miserable during family celebrations, you can agree as spouses to stick closer together. The point is to respond by drawing together rather than allowing pressure to split you apart.

BAD BEHAVIOR

Extended families may bring us into contact with behavior we don't approve of. Drunkenness, drug abuse, sex outside of marriage, homosexuality, swearing, violence, child abuse—these and other issues make family time uncomfortable or worse. You're not going to enjoy family events if you suspect Uncle Peter is a pedophile, or if everybody in the family except you considers Aunt June cute when she gets drunk and starts swearing a blue streak.

Your first concern should be your children's physical safety. You don't sacrifice their welfare on the altar of extended family.

For other kinds of bad behavior, though, the right response is less clear. Are you worried that your children will learn some bad words from Aunt June's filthy mouth? They probably can't learn anything that they don't hear at school. What about Uncle Rich, who brings his male partner to family gatherings? Unless Uncle Rich is taking your kids aside to indoctrinate them to his point of view, I doubt he's doing them harm. They will get exposed to homosexuality sooner or later. Wouldn't you rather dialogue with them as they learn about it in the context of family?

Some families feel that they need to express moral disapproval of their relatives' lifestyles. For example, they feel that they have to show disapproval of the couple who is living together unmarried, lest their children think that they don't care.

We have a right to confront immoral behavior. We certainly shouldn't get shamed into silence. However, we can express our views in many different ways, in private as well as in public. If we make a public fuss, people may get polarized and angry. Usually you're better off to talk about it in private. Timing and context matter. You can discuss these folks with your children when you get home, stating your convictions plainly but also teaching them the Christian art of rejecting the sin while loving and accepting the sinner.

FAMILY YOU DON'T LIKE

Immoral behavior isn't usually the issue. Personal differences are. We could easily foster family unity and love if not for one basic fact: lots of family members don't like each other. We're different. We don't always get along. Who wants to go to family reunions that seethe with tension because somebody arrived late? Who wants to hold family nights when children treat each other with genuine contempt? Plenty of people conclude that it is easier and better to look for love outside the family.

Yet I believe such difficulties are an essential part of families' glory. Yes, family members can be difficult. Guess what, so can all human beings. In families, we can learn how to be reconciled.

Unless you take very extreme measures to cut yourself off, your family members will be in your life forever. Friends may fight and split and be lost to each other for good. Once you lose touch, you may never see each other or hear of each other again. Not so with families. That means families give you many chances to make up for past affronts, to forget annoyances, to forgive and to be forgiven. Sometimes it takes a lifetime. With family, though, you have a lifetime.

Surely that is why God chose to redeem the world through a family: he needed the time. God knew that he would need generations of continuing contact to bring humanity back to himself. Just as Joseph and his brothers needed decades of simmering guilt and years of feints toward forgiveness, so God would need years by the thousands to get to reconciliation in Jesus in the fullness of time.

The implication for family is: keep trying. If you don't like each other, stay in touch and do the best you can. Sometimes counseling can be a great help. Look for opportunities to try a new approach. You can't force unity and love on people (or on yourself). You can keep in touch, keep praying—and keep watching for God at work.

8
SEXUAL FIDELITY
Seeing Sex God's Way

"You shall not commit adultery." EXODUS 20:14

"I tell you that anyone who divorces his wife, except for marital unfaithfulness, causes her to become an adulteress." MATTHEW 5:32

"Let us behave decently . . . not in orgies and drunkenness, not in sexual immorality and debauchery." ROMANS 13:13

"Among you there must not be even a hint of sexual immorality." EPHESIANS 5:3

"Marriage should be honored by all." HEBREWS 13:4

I doubt I have to convince you to care about sexual fidelity. Most parents care very much about their children's sexual behavior. In fact, it haunts them. Unwanted pregnancies, sexually transmitted diseases, pointless promiscuity, unhappy marriages—parents recognize these possibilities from the time their children are very small. By the time their children become teenagers, nightmares can keep parents awake at night.

Most parents remember their own youthful thoughts of sex, and they understand the temptations. They want their children to "be good," to stay out of trouble.

It is odd, therefore, that most parents find it hard to talk to their children about sex. They care immensely, but the subject makes them uniquely uncomfortable.

Unlike many people, I don't find sex particularly difficult to discuss. Over thirty years I have written a question-and-answer column in a magazine aimed at teenagers, *Campus Life*. Young people have written me every question imaginable about love and sex. After years of using words like *masturbation* and *orgasm*, I don't get so embarrassed.

I'm often amazed at how freely young people write to me, somebody they've never even met. They pour out their thoughts and experiences as though they were writing in a private diary. I have to remember, however, where young people learn about sexuality nowadays. They watch television. Television teaches them to talk publicly about anything and everything, and especially about sex. Think what you can overhear on a midday talk show!

Young people are not, contrary to what some parents fear, careless hedonists. Most want what their great-grandparents wanted from relationships. They seek deep, lifelong, soul-satisfying love, not a series of erotic encounters. (Although, of course, many wouldn't object to a series of erotic encounters along the way. Some of their great-grandparents felt that way too.)

They are unlike their great grandparents in this, however: most believe lifelong love is found by accident. Lifelong love is not based on a careful search and courtship. You meet somebody fabulous and— zing!—it happens. It works like that in the movies, doesn't it? Consequently, young people ask again and again how to be sure that they feel love, not just infatuation.

Their logic works this way: if this is really love, then it will last forever. If it's not really love, then the relationship is doomed to end in sadness. The tricky part is, how do you tell? Was that really a zing I felt, or was it just wishful thinking? Hundreds and hundreds of times I have been asked how to tell true love from infatuation, as though they were formed out of different substances, like gold and brass, that can be separated by a chemical analysis.

Young people really don't think they have much control over their love life. They expect love to happen to them, not for love to be nurtured and developed by them. How can you develop a zing?

With this mentality, sexual experimentation becomes very common. If you hope to get zinged, there is no more likely way than through sex. Parents should realize, though, that the vast majority of young people aren't just carelessly experimenting with sex. Plenty of careless flings happen, but underneath is a very serious search. They are hoping to discover the love of their life. Sex seems to be a reasonable way to carry on the search.

I'm amazed at how little help these young people get in developing a more effective approach. They get a lot of "teaching" from television, a lot from the movies, and almost nothing of substance from their churches and their parents. I suspect many parents are afraid they don't know the answers to their kids' questions.

If kids are to get any guidance on sexual values, they will probably have to get it from their parents. They won't get help from school (including most Christian schools). They won't get it from church. The typical church youth group talks about "relationships" but doesn't say much about sex. Even churches with very strong sexual standards rarely get around to talking about them. The subject is left to parents. If parents can't help their children develop core values for sexuality, they leave them to the kindly care of Hollywood.

WE NEED MORE THAN FACTS

Occasionally you'll see a newspaper article trumpeting the news—usually from Planned Parenthood or another organization dedicated to secular sex education—that young people have an appalling ignorance of sex. "A study has found that 78% of young people ages 15-19 can't answer basic questions about sex."

If you probe a little deeper, you'll find that many of the "basic questions" have to do with the biology of reproduction and the anatomy of sexual organs. Other questions might have to do with the prevalence of homosexuality or the statistical likelihood of pregnancy under certain conditions. The unstated proposition is that such biological ignorance causes grave problems like sexually transmitted diseases and unmarried pregnancies.

If those articles are correct in their assumptions, parents aren't going to be of much help teaching their children about sex. Biology scares parents. They're not sure they know all the correct names and biological functions that apply to sexuality. And even if they do, they feel out of their element—stupid and stumbling—when they try to talk about it.

Is ignorance at the heart of young people's sexual problems? Not really. In thirty years of answering kids' questions, I have found very few young people who lack basic biological information. They all know how you get pregnant, how you catch sexually transmitted diseases and what a condom is for. Their information may not be terribly detailed, but most of the time it's adequate. What they lack is information on how to live. They lack sensible, practical values regarding sex.

Ignorance is a secondary issue. To prove it, all you have to do is look at kids who know all the facts. Do they have problems with unmarried pregnancies and sexually transmitted diseases? Yes, they certainly do. Do kids who know all the facts stay out of trouble? Do they naturally form loving, lifelong marriages? They don't. Knowledge and values are not the same. They are not even necessarily related. Don't get me wrong. Knowledge is better than ignorance, but strong values trump them both.

I'm not talking about a list of dos and don'ts, either. Kids need guidance on what's right and wrong in particular situations, but that is only useful if they have values to undergird those guidelines. Rules about "how far to go" melt in the heat of passion unless a philosophy of "why" supports them. Some programs for youth spend a lot of time helping kids practice how to say no. That can be useful, but only for those who understand what they're saying yes to.

Young people need to understand that the Bible offers a fundamental "yes" for sexuality. Many think Scripture is very negative about sex. It's not so. The Bible has a few—very few—negative commands about sex, like warning signs on a construction zone. "Stay out of this area," the signs say. "It's full of danger."

Scripture is mainly positive. It advocates sexual faithfulness within marriage. "Husbands, love your wives, just as Christ loved the church" (Ephesians 5:25). Could the Bible make it any stronger or put it any more positively? That command is the flip side of the seventh commandment, "You shall not commit adultery." God wants to fulfill our deep human longings through loving, lifelong marriages.

Sexual faithfulness within marriage makes the foundation for everything else. Kids need to know this value and feel its importance. They may know the facts of life. They may have detailed guidelines for staying out of trouble. They may have parents who supervise their lives very carefully. That is all to the good, but it will do no good if the young people don't understand the fundamental attractiveness of sexual fidelity.

PREPARING FOR FAITHFULNESS

True, sexual fidelity doesn't make much obvious sense while you're a teenager. The same can be said of other core values. Take hard work. Exactly why, many a teenager has asked, should I study algebra? What is the point of doing chores? Hard work *isn't* a core value for children. It applies to adult life, which childhood must prepare us for.

Sexual fidelity is just the same. Children need to learn it and value it years before they get the benefit of it.

Yet faithfulness begins long before you meet the person you'll be faithful to. The old idea of "saving yourself" for marriage is correct. Virginity is a real and wonderful phenomenon. A virgin is different from a nonvirgin, is open and untouched, like "virgin" land. A virgin is radically ready to bond to another person in such a way that the bond will stick.

Sex is not merely a physical encounter. It is a spiritual act that makes a lasting mark on your life. In the ideal situation, your spouse makes that spiritual mark, as you adapt to each other in the intimacy and security of marriage. However, the majority of people today get marked by somebody else—quite likely somebody who now means nothing to them. As one girl wrote to me, "I have been changed by sex." Unfortunately, she had not been changed for the better, regarding her preparation for faithfulness to a lifelong partner.

The failure to stay sexually faithful before marriage makes it harder to stay sexually faithful in marriage. Having made and broken intimate bonds with other partners, people find it hard to bond anew and easier to keep a bit of a reserve on their commitment. Married couples can overcome this, just as they can overcome other kinds of hurts that they bring into marriage. How much better if they don't have to.

Like everybody else in America, I've seen some wonderful couples end up splitting. I've talked with them and prayed with them through counseling, reconciliation, separation, and then the final cold division of property and child custody. Like everybody else in America, I have had my heart broken by terrible blows delivered through the divorce courts.

Yet I don't believe that broken marriages are just the luck of the draw. I'm not convinced that divorce is inevitable in a certain percentage of marriages—and certainly not in 50 percent of marriages, which is approximately the current failure rate. Not every marriage can be saved, I grant. Sometimes one or both partners has suffered such a terrible history, carries such a load of trauma or has such a hardened heart that nothing human can help. However, I've also seen impossible marriages saved. What kept them alive through the crisis was a deep habit of faithfulness built into the lives of the two partners (and their friends and families). What enabled them to emerge together from the crisis, battle-hardened and newly committed, was also the deep habit of faithfulness.

A faithful marriage is difficult even under the best circumstances. People who never practice faithfulness before they're married find it doubly difficult. They live like free agents until they meet their partner-for-life. Then they're supposed to become as faithful as a golden retriever. There's a complete disconnect between the values of youth and the values of married life.

Here, I believe, family culture can make a crucial difference. Family culture can teach the value of faithfulness, so that even small children begin to think of it and participate in it.

SHOW-AND-TELL FIDELITY

The best way to teach sexual fidelity is to live it. When kids see parents who are faithful to each other, they understand it as the norm. And they want to experience it for themselves. Sexual fidelity is an ideal that still appeals to those who have seen it lived.

Fidelity is more than the absence of adultery. It's the unswerving devotion of sexual partners to each other's welfare. It's the willingness of a partner to stop his or her headlong assertion of self and put the other's concerns first. It's the commitment to get along, even when it takes compromise and self-control. It's a demonstration of love that is clear and pointed, rather than assumed. Above all, it's the will to forgive offenses and overlook faults.

You should make sure to practice these qualities in front of your children. Let them see the reality of marriage, even when marriage is hard! Most couples have a few rituals by which they express their love. Make sure your children get to participate! If you give roses for Valentines, involve your children in picking out the flowers. If you make a special meal-for-two on your anniversary, consider whether your children could participate in the preparation or the serving.

I've already mentioned one family ritual, the parents' weekend away. Children may put up a fuss when they're left behind, but underneath they like knowing that their parents love each other. They learn an important lesson about faithful married partners: they put their relationship first, even ahead of their children. This carves into young minds the idea that they too will want such a faithful relationship.

Naturally, every couple shows faithfulness in their own way. Some like moonlight and roses and *Sonnets from the Portuguese;* others prefer installing a new kitchen floor. Whatever your style, make a point of letting your children see it, and get them to participate wherever you can.

Model Couples

Single parents may think they have no way to demonstrate sexual fidelity, but that is not really true. You demonstrate faithfulness through your choice of dating partners—or your willingness to go without dates when the right kind of person isn't available. You demonstrate fidelity through the way you conduct yourself on dates, and through your chaste behavior. Don't think for a minute that your children don't see! They learn how to relate romantically through watching how you relate romantically.

All the same, single parents can't model a faithful marriage. If they're divorced, they may have unhealthy patterns to live down. Many find it extremely helpful when other families befriend them, so that good models of faithful marriage can be part of their kids' everyday life.

Even if you're not a single parent, your children can benefit from seeing other marriages up close. So choose your friends thoughtfully! My children, for example, gained a lot from the example of their youth pastor and his wife. They were a lot closer in age to my kids—and a whole lot cooler.

TAKING ROMANCE SERIOUSLY

More than seeing adults' faithfulness is involved, though: from an early age children can begin to understand faithfulness in their own lives. Author and professor Donald Joy emphasizes the importance of treating even grade-school crushes respectfully. For example, parents can ask for updates on the latest girlfriend/boyfriend and—rather than smiling at the answers—treat them seriously. As older people we may know that this young love won't last, but to the person involved it feels very serious! When we treat it respectfully we communicate that relationships at the age of eight or eighteen matter—as indeed they do. The way people relate in grade school has some bearing on how they will relate when they're adults.

More than that, grade school crushes form the beginnings of the Great Romance—the search for and cultivation of a lifelong love.

There are other ways to take the Great Romance seriously. Some families celebrate their wedding anniversaries by repeatedly telling the story of how they met and fell in love. Some like to ask guests and family friends to do the same when they visit. Most children enjoy these stories of love, because they match their own sense of romantic adventure. By telling these stories we reinforce the wonder at how two people find each other, fall in love and marry. From a very young age children can catch this spirit and believe that one special relationship can come to them.

Some books and movies capture this spirit. *Little Women* has played a role in millions of young girls' lives, partly to build their faith and hope in love. Jane Austen's wonderful novels, also rendered in several excellent films, circle around the hope for love and marriage in a cynical and discouraging world. So does the chick flick *Sleepless in Seattle*. In a far lighter vein, *The Princess Bride* is a film that takes an adventurous but fond look at the motive power of love—and it is a film that appeals to boys.

You will, no doubt, have your own favorites. They can easily become family favorites, reference points in your family culture. Make sure you don't choose equally romantic favorites that glamorize infidelity. There are many of these. I'm not suggesting that you never watch *Casablanca*. Just be aware that you're not building faith in fidelity.

Many people encourage young people to begin praying for their future spouse. This means imagining the person existing (which he or she probably does) and also imagining the kind of life you hope he or she will lead in these years before you meet. Of course this leads naturally to considering the kind of life *you* should lead, with faithfulness to that future spouse in mind.

Some families pray for each member of the family on his or her birthday. I think you can include prayers for a possible future spouse.

"Dates" with Parents

Some families have regular "dates" with their children—dads with their daughters, mothers with their sons. They try to create the intimacy of a real date, treating each other in a special way. Partly they are creating positive conversation between parents and child, particularly after adolescence has reared up and bedtime stories are no longer in order. Partly too, they do elementary training in how men and women like to treat each other. They give instructions on how to open doors, help with coats, use proper table manners and carry on conversation. They're not only preparing their children for true dating, they're emphasizing the concern and gentility that should characterize relations between the sexes. Knowing how to treat a man or woman as a special and valued creature helps lay the groundwork for faithful relationships.

"THE TALK"

Every child needs to learn—and will learn—the facts of life. The only questions are when and from what source. I always wanted my children to learn from my wife and me. Most parents do, I think. That is why you should have The Talk by about the age of eight—earlier in some cases. Most parents think that is too young, until their son or daughter is ten or twelve and they begin to realize they may have missed their best opportunity. Eight is a very approachable age. Beyond the age of eight the odds get very high that your son or daughter will learn about the birds and bees from some other source.

The purpose of The Talk is not an education in sexology. Most kids, I suspect, remain very fuzzy about details even after The Talk. The purpose of The Talk is to open the door for more discussions—discussions that will build belief in faithfulness.

Here's how we did The Talk. When our children reached the age of eight, they knew it was time to have a special night with Mom or Dad. At least, the boys knew it, after their sister led the way. Boys went with Dad, girls with Mom. I don't believe the sexual division of labor was absolutely necessary, but it was convenient. I'm sure a single mom or dad could handle this chore with a child of the opposite sex.

We put the emphasis on fun. We went to a nice hotel for the night, with plans to do whatever activity the child chose. My daughter Katie wanted to go swimming in the hotel pool; my son Chase chose to hit baseballs. We ate at a nice restaurant of the child's choice.

First, though, after checking into the hotel, we got out a cartoon book that explained sexual intercourse and reproduction in a light-hearted but accurate way. (You can find such books in any good bookstore. Just be sure to read it yourself ahead of time.) We read through it together and then took time to talk about it. Some children are very curious and have lots of questions; others take the information in a matter-of-fact way. At the age of eight, sex is a fairly impersonal discussion for most children. (For parents, of course, it's intensely personal. The Talk is much harder on parents' nerves than on children's.)

My personal opinion is that The Talk should go light on anatomy lessons. Basic differences between a penis and a vagina should be explained, as should the whereabouts and shape of sperm and egg. Make sure you move quickly to the main subject, though: sexual intercourse. It can be described in lay terms. You don't need to explain how it feels, except to say that sex is a wonderful experience. Explain that Moms and Dads do it often because they like to, and that in doing so they bring sperm and egg together to make a baby.

We made sure to tell our children that they would probably have more questions later on. We told them we would leave the book on the bookshelf in case they wanted to look at it some more, and we would be glad to talk more whenever they wanted to.

After we talked, we went out to play. It was a special parent-child night together. They had looked forward to it. We felt relieved that we got through it. (As I said, I'm accustomed to talking about sex, but with my own children the subject remains nerve-wracking.)

I want to emphasize that for our family no earthshaking conversations took place during The Talk. Of course, a great exchange could occur, but don't count on it. Few eight-year-olds are deeply invested in reproduction and sex. Eight-year-olds are old enough to understand the subject, but they are not emotionally involved the way they will be when puberty arrives.

The Talk normalizes the topic and gets all the explosive information on the table before the subject gets edgy. I recommend checking in a week or two later. "Did any more thoughts or questions come up after we had our talk last week?" After that you'll find it relatively simple to carry on further conversation. Innumerable opportunities arise—when you're watching a TV show, or when family members have marital difficulties. You can be as candid as you want to be, because the subjects that scare kids and their parents are already out in the open.

The Talk need not say much about faithfulness in marriage. I think it is enough to say that God designed sex for married people to enjoy. Most eight-year-olds aren't thinking about sexual ethics, and a heavyweight talk will only go over their heads. You'll have plenty of chances to talk about faithfulness—and unfaithfulness—because life will bring situations to you.

Preparing for Adolescence

James Dobson has produced a book and audio series for parents to use with children on the verge of adolescence. Many parents have used it as the basis of a private weekend away with their kids. I think of *Preparing for Adolescence* as an update of The Talk. Twelve is an extremely vulnerable age for many children, quite different from the age of eight, which is generally a sunny and stable period in the growth of a child. *Preparing for Adolescence* brings the dialogue about sexuality into a new context, where the subject is no longer theoretical. Most twelve-year-olds are still too young to have practical ethical questions, but unlike eight-year-olds they can actually feel the compelling attraction of the opposite sex. The dark and mysterious allure of sexuality enters their lives at about this point. Their bodies begin to change as well.

You can "update" adolescence in other ways. For years Popie and I taught a week-long summer class for rising seventh graders, in which we talked about a Christian view of sex along with the issues that our students would soon be exposed to in middle school. One of the most important aspects of that week was the "homework" papers we sent home. Students were assigned to interview their parents, asking them how they fell in love, what attracted them to their spouse, how they learned the facts of life, and various other topics. We hoped to encourage open-ended dialogue between parents and children, and I think we often did.

Dialogue between parents and children typically gets harder at this age, but that doesn't make it any less important. The facts of life need updating for a new period of life. Sometimes it takes a set program like *Preparing for Adolescence* to open up the conversation.

Screening Media

Television and movies have a unique ability to swallow us whole. They create a dream world that seems more real than life.

That makes television and movies hugely entertaining, but also a huge source of manipulation. A good director can make black seem white. People who are repelled and horrified by adultery in real life find themselves rooting for the actors onscreen to dump their stultifying spouses and dive into bed. Video can make you believe that old lie, "It was destiny!"

Children lack life experiences to counter such images. Most find television and movies extremely engrossing. What they see in the movies may be the most "real" life experience they've had! If movies show them that sex is the most compellingly beautiful result of infatuation, they will know it to be true. If they get a pornographic image planted in their minds, it will stick. Some visual images are so strong they overpower, dominating any other point of view.

Some families try to fend off the media entirely, staying away from all TV and movies. Most do something trickier: screening what their children see.

Part of the trickiness lies in this: different families have different standards. In fact, different parents in the same family will have different standards. What I find horrible you will find only mildly troubling, and vice versa. I'm regularly amazed at what some wonderful families allow their children to see. And I'm fairly sure other families are amazed at what I allow *my* children to see.

The Internet can be helpful in making decisions about particular movies. Several parental guidance websites give detailed descriptions of the content of virtually every popular movie and video. A rating of PG-13 doesn't tell you much, especially since language, violence and sexual content are all lumped together to make one broad rating. You'll often see it differently than the ratings board did. If you read up on the movie via a parental guidance website, you'll have a pretty accurate idea what specific scenes the movie includes.

I'm sorry to say, however, that few parents manage invariably to do careful research in advance. Most families fall back on using those general ratings—G, PG, PG-13 and R—as their standard, and then they make exceptions in individual cases. When our children were teenagers, they were allowed to watch PG-13 but not R movies. We made exceptions, but only when we had seen the movie ourselves in advance. We didn't make exceptions just because our kids begged us to.

No matter what standards you hold, they will almost surely be

tested. Your children will want to see something forbidden, if only because their friends are seeing it. This conflict, while unpleasant, is actually necessary and beneficial. The conflict gives you a wonderful chance
to teach sexual values.

Let me explain. If you don't have a set of standards, the line of argu-
ment will go like this. "Why can't I see *Red-Hot Honeys*? Rodney got to
see it. All my friends got to see it! It's really popular! How do you know
there's anything wrong with it? Rodney said it was fine."

Unless you've seen the movie yourself (which is unlikely) or you have
time to look it up on a website (which time may not allow), you'll feel a
vague uncertainty. You won't like the title, but you know well enough
that Hollywood often uses deceptive titles. Should you follow your instinct and say no, based on the title, the newspaper ad and the trailer you
saw? Or will you give in just this once? In real life, your decision may
center on a test of wills. How much does your child want to see this
movie? If there's a lot of pleading or whining, will you give in? The only
way to find out is to try. Your child will certainly try, if he or she thinks
there's any chance of success.

If you keep strict standards, on the other hand, the battles will focus
on the standards, not some vague information about the contents of the
movie.

"Why can't I go to an R movie? You let me go to *The Brave and the
Reckless*."

"That was because I had seen *The Brave and the Reckless*, and I thought
it was fine. But the rule is, if it's an R, I have to see it first."

"But why? Some R-rated movies are fine."

"Yes, but most of them aren't, and those ratings, as flawed as they are,
remain the best way I know to judge a movie I haven't seen. If you can
come up with a better standard, that would be fine."

"Why do we need to have these rules anyway?"

"Because movies affect people deeply. I want to keep you from seeing
something that will leave lasting memories that hurt you."

Battles will surely come. Friends with different standards will invite
your children for a sleepover or a movie night. If you have standards,

you'll insist on knowing what the movie will be. You may even have to tell the other parents about your standards, to the intense annoyance and embarrassment of your child. Your standards may be right, or they may not fit well when applied to a particular movie. That's not the point. The point is that you have standards. Sexuality is important to you. You take movies seriously. The reason you don't want your child seeing certain kinds of sexual images is that you believe those images can hurt his or her ability to be faithful sexually in the course of life.

Of course, no set of standards can guarantee to keep your child from all questionable films or shows. Standards can improve the fare quite a lot, but ratings are imprecise, and some movies demonstrate extremely destructive views even if they're not graphically indecent. For my money, many regular TV shows have terrifically corrosive views of sex and relationships, even though they don't show any skin. If you're going to screen the media, you're sure to have breakdowns. Your kids will get exposed to material you don't think they should see. You need dialogue, regular dialogue about the messages seen. That's why you need to have The Talk—so you can begin open conversation.

INTERNET PORNOGRAPHY

I feel very strongly that children and young people should have their Internet content censored. Internet pornography is utterly destructive of a healthy and hopeful attitude toward sex. It not only demeans women, it demeans human beings. The less exposure children and young adults have to Internet porn, the better for them.

Pornography is so pervasive on the Internet that people hardly need to go looking for it. If they spend any time at all surfing the web, pornography will find them. To counteract this, some families keep the computer in plain view of the household, so there's little chance for private viewing. But will you always be there to supervise? As an alternative to personal supervision, Internet filters work quite well. Don't believe the articles that critique them for their imprecision. Yes, they do sometimes block sites unnecessarily, but parents can always go around the blockage, in the event that your children are kept from sites that they really need to see. Most Internet filters cost money, but the expense is well worth it.

SUPERVISING DATING

In older times, parents felt responsible to see that their children stayed out of trouble when they were together. Chaperones were a practical response to sexual temptation. A young man who wanted to court a young woman was expected to meet her parents, to show his honorable intentions. Parents were involved at every point in the process.

Practices like these went out with the '57 Ford, but recently some families have been trying to pull them back. "Courting" is the word some use to describe it. Parents require young men to meet them and declare their seriousness. They strongly discourage casual dating, believing that dating should be a very serious prelude to marriage. These parents want to be fully involved in their children's lives. They don't believe "this is none of your business."

As one who has lived in a country where parents still exercise full veto power over their children's relationships, I have to report that no amount of parental involvement guarantees good marriages. I don't believe God has ordained any particular method of courtship. I do think parents should get involved with their children's dating and not buy the idea that it is completely the kids' concern. Getting to know the person who is dating your child is a very minimal requirement. You have undoubtedly gained some wisdom about the world of romance. You can help guide your children through their relationships with the opposite sex.

Do not, therefore, let your children stonewall you when you ask about their date. Questions about where they went, with whom and what they did are quite appropriate. Furthermore, I wouldn't let any relationship go too far without getting to know the opposite party. If he or she can't stop by to get acquainted over a bowl of ice cream, he or she probably isn't the ideal partner for your child. If you have to insist, do. Parents are still in charge!

You probably can't prevent all heartache, but you can at least join in conversation with your child about the character needed in a potential partner. These conversations may not be easy, but they can help greatly in teaching the value of sexual fidelity.

SEXUAL FAILINGS

Some people will hate reading this chapter because it makes them so uncomfortable—even miserable. Many people feel deeply saddened by the mistakes they made when they were younger. Many feel haunted by their sexual failings in the present! And nearly all parents feel some guilt for not talking to their children the way they think they should. Embarrassment and discomfort overwhelm them.

I've had many parents ask me how they can talk to their children about sex, since they haven't lived spotless lives themselves. I'm always surprised that they see this as an obstacle. Would they refuse to talk to their children about being tardy to class if they themselves had a poor attendance record in school? Would they neglect to warn their children that shoplifting was wrong if they themselves had been caught stealing twenty years before? What is it about sex that makes us believe we have to be spotless in order to be helpful to our children? We're all the more qualified to give warnings when we've been there ourselves.

I have had some good role models for marriage, including my parents. I may have learned more, though, from couples for whom marriage was obviously a strain—if not a war zone. Those couples shared their pain, and I learned from it.

I learned from those painful marriages that something great is something worth suffering for. I learned that sexual fidelity often comes at great cost. I learned the heroism of marriage.

I offer this as encouragement for those who struggle in their marriages and whose thoughts about sexual fidelity are dominated by guilt. I wouldn't advocate confessing all your sins and doubts to children. They have enough worries without taking on yours. But you don't have to lie to your children, either. Without going into uncomfortable detail about your past, you can tell them that sexual fidelity is difficult but worth fighting for.

GOOD BOOKS

Here are some books I recommend as very helpful.

Where Did I Come From?
Peter Mayle, Carol Publishing Group
A cartoon book that communicates the facts of life in a breezy, light-hearted manner. Mayle offers no values, Christian or otherwise, but his book offers a positive view of sex and helps parents tell kids what they need to know.

How & When to Tell Your Kids About Sex
Stan and Brenna Jones, NavPress
Advice for parents from a leading Christian social scientist and his wife.

God's Design for Sex
Stan and Brenna Jones, NavPress
A series of four different books to read to children. Each book is aimed at a different age group, beginning at three years old.

Preparing for Adolescence
James Dobson, Word
Designed for parents and children to read together as the children approach the teenage years.

9
GENEROSITY
God's Irrational Exuberance

"Give to everyone who asks you, and if anyone takes what belongs to you, do not demand it back." LUKE 6:30

"We want you to know about the grace that God has given the Macedonian churches. . . . They gave as much as they were able, and even beyond their ability." 2 CORINTHIANS 8:1, 3

"Give, and it will be given to you. A good measure, pressed down, shaken together and running over, will be poured into your lap. For with the measure you use, it will be measured to you." LUKE 6:38

"Whoever sows generously will also reap generously."
2 CORINTHIANS 9:6

"God loves a cheerful giver." 2 CORINTHIANS 9:7

I remember a walk I took with an older Christian man while I was a student in college. Spring was in the air, green shoots spurted from every branch, and flowering trees threw sprays of color into the sky. Life seemed riotous, a divine splurge. We passed through a small park with a fountain dribbling a slow splash of water into a basin.

"Notice the generosity of God, and the frugality of man," my friend said, indicating the contrast between exploding plants and trickling fountain.

I have often thought back to that image, especially in springtime. Humans must treat their resources conservatively. We don't want to waste water, electricity or money. We have only so much, and we have to dole it out wisely or we'll run out. God, however, is a spendthrift. In springtime he splurges on tadpoles, carpets his fields with wildflowers, fills whole trees with blossoms and bumblebees. Birds provide continuous music over thousands of square miles.

God shows the same generosity in relating to us personally. He acts irrationally, exuberantly, in our favor. "If God is for us, who can be against us? He who did not spare his own Son, but gave him up for us all—how will he not also, along with him, graciously give us all things?" (Romans 8:31-32). He gives us far more than we deserve, and far better.

God's program—his kingdom plan, if you will—seeks to create a society where everybody reflects his glory. His glory shines in his generosity, that splurging, spontaneous demonstration of love. Therefore he wants to make us generous—generous like him.

Do you want to raise generous kids? Most Christians feel their hearts warm when they see kindergartners share their toys, or when a teenager wants to contribute his allowance to help a needy family. That is only part of the picture, though. Generosity as the Bible describes it, and as God lives it, shows dangerous tendencies. True generosity exceeds common sense. It seems wasteful—and it is wasteful, if you are thinking in human terms.

GENEROUS RISKS

To talk seriously about generosity we have to start with money and property, because generosity gets immediately practical at that point. Jesus said, "Where your treasure is, there your heart will be also" (Matthew 6:21). When you learn to be generous with your stuff—with your car keys, your bank account, your precious power tools—you break the back of the miser in his heart. Generosity is more than a benevolent feeling. Generosity is action.

Yet generosity must also involve the spirit. You can tithe your income, carefully and calculatedly planning your gifts. You can write large checks, taking care that your money gets used well by various charities. Some people would call that generous. I would not. Planned giving is well and good, but generosity goes beyond calculation. Generosity takes risks. Generosity doesn't throw money away, but it throws it around.

Randy Alcorn suggests a thought experiment in his book *Money, Possessions and Eternity.* Suppose, he says, you are a financial counselor. An elderly woman comes in whose husband died six years ago. "I'm down to my last two dollars," she says. "Yet I feel like I should put the whole two dollars in the church offering. What do you think?"

Then suppose a middle-aged man comes into your office. A very successful farmer, he has a question about his business. "The farm is doing well, and I see a chance to make a significant profit if I can hold my crops until prices go up. I've got a plan to invest in another storage facility. If all goes well I'll be able to take it easy, retire early, maybe do some traveling and have a good time. What do you think?"

Most people would tell the widow to hold on to her money. She needs it; the church does not. Most people would congratulate the farmer on his good business plan. Alcorn points out, however, that Jesus reacted differently, contradicting the advice of every financial planner in the universe. Jesus commended the poor widow for her generosity (Mark 12:43-44). In giving away her last dollar, she exceeded the generosity of the biggest philanthropist in the city, and so she could serve as an example for all Jesus' disciples. Of the farmer, Jesus said, "You fool!" (Luke 12:20). His plans were defective because he was one of those people who "stores up things for himself but is not rich toward God" (12:21).

Jesus favored generosity. So did the first generation of Christians. Swept up by the Holy Spirit, believers spontaneously sold their property in Jerusalem so that the proceeds could be given out to anybody in the church who had needs (Acts 4:34-35). When Paul praised the Macedonian Christians for giving "beyond their ability" (2 Corinthians 8:1-3), he was recognizing generosity that exceeded common sense.

Generosity cannot be commanded. You can't make enough rules and guidelines to create a generous spirit. Does the government create a generous nation through high taxation? Does a parent teach a child to be generous by setting down strict rules for sharing her toys? No, generosity must be self-motivated, unforced, spontaneous.

Generosity cannot be forced, but it can be inspired. Generosity is so joyful, so fun, that people catch it like the flu. If you get near it, you feel drawn into it. So most people catch generosity from a family member or a friend. (They catch uptight, upright, calculating conservatism in the same way.) Family culture is the most natural way to encourage generosity—and maybe the only way.

Do you want to raise generous kids? Then you have to create a family culture of generosity. You have to become generous yourself, in such a way that the whole family shares in that spirit.

NOT COMPLETELY STINGY

Generosity is hard for me. Generosity is hard for most people, which I suspect explains why Jesus put so much stress on the way we handle material possessions. It divides people between those who are willing to let go and follow God and those who insist on keeping control.

I feel that divide every time a homeless person asks me for spare change. Having enough money isn't the issue. If I put a five-dollar bill in the hand of every homeless person I met, the total wouldn't amount to much. I'm worried more that I'm wasting the money. I know very well that my spare change stands an excellent chance of taking a shortcut to the nearest liquor store.

But my concerns go even deeper than that rational consideration. For some reason I feel myself withdrawing from the homeless person, not wanting to look him or her in the eye, show human feeling or take time to talk. I don't want to walk to the nearest grocery store to buy some food for the homeless person. I don't want to talk with the man on the sidewalk to see if I can get any sense of what's up in his life. In some respects my sensible explanations about wasting money only cover up a deeper fact. I'm not generous. Something inside me bristles at the thought of giving away money to someone who might blow it. I only want to help if I get an iron-clad guarantee the help won't be misused.

I don't want to give the impression that I'm completely stingy. Really,

I'm not. I'm better at writing checks. Giving to charity always has an element of risk in it, since you can't be sure the money will get used in the absolutely most effective way conceivable. I do some research and pick responsible agencies, to minimize my risk.

I'm not totally stingy, but I'm ambivalent about generosity. Most people are, and it comes out when they raise their kids. We parents battle to get them to think ahead. We want them to plan, to think through consequences, not to waste money or to be careless with possessions. So we react when we see our children acting generous. I can't easily tell what is carelessness and what is real generosity. (Especially since kids are generous with possessions that we, the parents, provide.)

For example, I remember a period when my daughter Katie gave lots of kids rides home from school. She sacrificed a significant chunk of her time, and she burned up a lot of gas. Rather than congratulating her on her generosity, I felt immediate concern that other kids were taking advantage of her.

We parents take risks when we let our children act generous. We must accept that some of our hard-earned money might be wasted. In fact, we can be sure it will. That is the cost of generosity.

When I lived in Kenya I thought a lot about the risks of generosity. Genuinely hungry and needy people lived near me in vast numbers. Yet plenty of crooks and swindlers also worked on guilt-stricken, compassionate Westerners. They typically concentrated on tourists, but sometimes they got me too. With such great needs so close and real, these swindles struck me as obscene. I hated to discover that I'd been taken. Yet I couldn't always tell the real thing from the fake—sometimes not even long afterwards.

My choice came to this: either I had to stop giving altogether, or I had to accept that whenever I gave to anybody, I took a chance on being conned. I eventually arrived at this maxim: "I would rather be cheated a hundred times than have a heart of stone."

I think Jesus would say just that. After all, that widow who gave her last two dollars put the money into the temple treasury, to be spent by the high priest and his bureaucracy. We could all suggest better charities!

However, when Jesus evaluated what she did, he wasn't thinking about the temple bureaucracy. He thought of that woman's heart. Her untamed generosity mattered far more than the efficient use of two dollars. Jesus saw her act as beautiful.

We want our children to learn to think, to plan, to use money wisely. That's all good. Generosity is even better.

TEACH ABOUT GOD'S OWNERSHIP

The classic idea of stewardship is based on the belief that everything in the universe belongs to God. He merely gives us some of his estate to take care of on his behalf. We can afford to be generous—it's not our stuff! We know the wild generosity of the Owner, and that should encourage us to be generous with his property.

Jesus told several stories that teach this idea very dramatically. You can talk through these stories with your children. Some of the most important are:

"Canceled Debts" (Luke 7:41-43). The bigger the forgiven debt, the greater love inspired.

"The Shrewd Manager" (Luke 16:1-8). If you want to have friends, you can start by treating them better than they deserve.

"The Talents" (Matthew 25:14-30). When a master leaves his servants in charge of his estate, he doesn't want them to be too conservative. Rather, take risks!

"Unmerciful Servant" (Matthew 18:23-35). Let people off easy if you want your master to let you off too.

"Workers in the Vineyard" (Matthew 20:1-15). If some people get extra pay, what's it to you?

All these stories are quirky, and easy and obvious "morals" are scarce. The stories provoke your imagination about the unusual—not to say outrageous—behavior God wants to see in us.

Involve Your Children in Charitable Giving

The first and most obvious way to raise generous children is to let them see you acting generously. For many of us, regular donations to charities make up the core of this.

As I've already mentioned, you can invite children into a family discussion of which organizations to give to. Even more powerfully, you can invite them to share in the adventure of generosity. For example, discuss a challenge to increase your family giving by one percentage point a year—and monitor your progress throughout the year. That lets the kids enjoy the thrill of trying to outdo themselves in giving.

Your sharing might involve a bit of sacrifice—beans and rice once a month, say, in order to send money to feed AIDS orphans in Uganda the only protein-rich meal of their week.

Or, invite them to a discussion of one "over-the-top" gift that you'll make at the end of the year (or the end of each month, if you're brave enough). If children propose something outrageous, go with it—explore with them what it would cost to make that kind of gift. Work it through with them, and show yourself willing to let them lead you into genuine, sacrificial generosity. Scared? Maybe you should be, but I doubt anybody ever starved to death by playing this game.

Random Acts of Kindness

Some people take pleasure from paying the toll for the car behind them in line, buying movie tickets for a family of strangers waiting their turn or distributing extra pastries in a coffee shop. Do something extra like this with your kids, and I guarantee they won't forget it! Somebody may object that random kindness is pointless, but if so, why does God do it so often?

Pick Up Litter

Everybody knows they shouldn't litter, but how often do you see somebody pick up after people they don't even know? I remember going for a walk with my friend Jack. We encountered some broken glass on the walkway, and before I even knew it Jack had stooped down and begun picking it up. I was stunned. I hadn't broken the glass; why should I pick it up? To avoid embarrassment, though, I joined in the cleanup—and never forgot the unforced generosity of my friend Jack.

In every public place you'll find litter. It offers you virtually unlimited opportunities for small generous acts. Your kids may be bemused or even embarrassed by a parent who does what nobody else does, but they will remember!

LEND YOUR POSSESSIONS

For some people no act of generosity comes harder than lending stuff, because they're emotionally attached to their possessions and can't let go. Something seizes up inside at the thought of letting your new car go on the church ski trip or lending your power tools to the group going to Mexico to build houses. The car may get dented. The tools may get lost or broken. However, such tangible acts of generosity make sense to children in a way that the abstract writing of checks might not.

We made it a family policy, when we bought a new minivan, to make it available to the church or school anytime they needed it. And they needed it frequently! We sent a full minivan to Mexico, into the Sierra for ski trips, and to a great variety of other destinations. I almost always found it a little hard to let the car out of my hands. However, I am quite sure my children will remember these small acts of generosity and want to imitate them.

Typical of any writer, Randy Alcorn has a thing for books. He reasoned, though, that in his church's library the books would remain available to him whenever he needed them, and others would be able to use them as well. So he gave all his books away. He reports, "Though I still love books, my emotional attachment to possessing them is gone." I wonder how his children were changed by watching him.

DEVELOP CHRISTMAS RITUALS

Christmas offers opportunities for family rituals expressing generosity. For example, you can develop a habit of dropping money into every Salvation Army kettle you encounter, encouraging the kids to keep a sharp eye out for them. Let the kids decide how much to give each time. Keep track of how much you have given, and try to set a new record each Christmas.

Some organizations offer opportunities to give presents to needy children. In my community we have a program called the Christmas angel tree. You pick a card off a Christmas tree. The card describes a present "wished for" by a needy child of a certain age. After you buy and wrap the present, you place the gift under the tree.

You can easily make this a family ritual, letting each member of the family choose a present and then comparing notes as to what you bought. Don't set a price limit. See how generous you can be!

GIVE TO ANYONE WHO ASKS

Families can also determine to give something—always—to anybody who asks for help. Maybe money isn't the answer. Try food. Some people keep food in the car for just such opportunities. Making this a family custom will help you build up each other and create a family culture of generosity.

CREATE OPPORTUNITIES FOR SHARING

Sharing isn't exactly generosity, but sharing moves you in the right direction. You can imagine a progression: from a two-year-old who grabs at other children's toys to a child who feels it's natural to share those toys, to a child who thinks first of others and gets joy from seeing them get what they want. Nobody gets from the first stage to the third without going through the middle one, learning how to share.

In our affluent society, some parents provide so bountifully that their children never have to share. Each one has his own room. Each child has plenty of toys of her own. That's not necessarily good. Providing so well for your children may, in effect, turn them into selfish people.

Some families deliberately bring out a limited supply of toys, to make sharing necessary. Some produce a limited supply of cookies. They deliberately create situations that must be negotiated, rather than choosing the peace and quiet that come from parent-imposed fairness.

SEND AN EXTRA SNACK

When your child takes a bag lunch, you can add an extra cookie "to share with somebody." Later you can ask whom your child shared the cookie with. That way you build the habit of generosity.

NATURALLY SELFISH CREATURES

Children are not naturally generous. Most parents get weary and disgusted trying to sort out quarrels between greedy and selfish children. I can remember the relief that came to our family when we replaced our Toyota with a minivan. When the children sat close enough to touch, they were bound to fight! The only solution was to give them enough separation—ideally, about a hundred yards. (So much for my idea of creating conditions for sharing.)

Teaching generosity to naturally selfish creatures requires huge outlays in energy and time. Of course, it also means rethinking your own life, since adults are not naturally generous either.

And don't expect much help from the society we live in. In theory people admire generosity, but when it gets too close to them they suddenly see many reasons for caution. Give sandwiches to the poor and people will treat your family with respect. Invite the poor home to dinner and the same people may start questioning whether their children should play at your house.

So you have to ask yourself: Do I want to raise generous children—children who reflect God's splurging and risky generosity? It will not happen by accident. You have to take steps.

There is a payoff, though, expressed in that old saying, "You can't outgive God." As Jesus put it, "Give, and it will be given to you" (Luke 6:38). Generosity seems risky and possibly irrational, when we think that the world is limited to what we see. Beyond what we see, however, romps a God who is extravagantly generous. Take the leap into generosity, and you begin to experience him and his economy.

10

SUBMISSION

Fitting into the Universe

"Blessed are those who are persecuted because of righteousness."
MATTHEW 5:10

*"Do not be proud, but be willing to associate with
people of low position."* ROMANS 12:16

"Submit to one another out of reverence for Christ." EPHESIANS 5:21

"Let your gentleness be evident to all." PHILIPPIANS 4:5

"Obey your leaders and submit to their authority." HEBREWS 13:17

"Is any one of you in trouble? . . . Pray." JAMES 5:13

*"Humble yourselves . . . under God's mighty hand,
that he may lift you up in due time."* 1 PETER 5:6

Americans find submission hard to swallow. We are a people trained in democracy, taught to believe that each person must think independently and rule his own life. Submitting to anything or anyone rankles us. "Who made *him* king of America?"

The Bible's basic view on submission, however, can be summarized in the words of Bob Dylan: "You gotta serve somebody." In different roles, in different times and places, everybody has to submit. Properly understood, submission doesn't make you subservient, nor does it make you lose your independence. It shows that you know how to fit into the universe.

Consider a restaurant. When you enter and sit down, you submit to the authority of the waitress or waiter. In your mind the server may be beneath you, but in many important respects, authority runs in the opposite direction. The server tells you where to sit, decides when and how to take your order, and brings you your food and drink in the manner he or she deems appropriate. You may consider these efforts poorly done, but you still don't get out of your seat and try to do it yourself. If you do, someone will ask you to sit down and submit to the server's proper authority. If the server does a capable job, everyone will get food in a timely and gracious fashion.

When you join an athletic team, you submit to the coach. On a job you submit to the boss. In a parking lot you submit to the attendants. Submission is really not controversial. Everyone must do it in certain times and places.

Humility is the character trait that produces proper submission. True, the word *humility* has gained a bad reputation. To some people it suggests groveling, in the manner of Dickens's slimy character Uriah Heep, "a very 'umble person."

Genuine humility is quite different. People who constantly devalue themselves probably just want attention. Genuinely humble people rank themselves just where they belong, not too high or too low. They can take the lowest job, if that needs doing, and not feel demoralized. Humble people can also take the lead where appropriate, and feel no sense of superiority. Humble people don't worry about their status. They care about getting work done in the best way possible. When that requires submission, no problem.

The fact that I submit to a server in a restaurant does not mean that I am inferior to the server. If the server plays on the softball team I coach, our roles are reversed. The server submits to me. We must both move smoothly between submission and leadership, depending on the situation.

THE MOST NOTORIOUS EXAMPLE
The most notorious example of submission comes in the apostle Paul's

advice to wives. He told them to submit to their husbands (Ephesians 5:22). Did he mean that female submission in marriage is intrinsically necessary because of the God-given nature of male and female? Or was he giving situational advice, urging Christians to live peacefully within the locally agreed-on expectations of Greco-Roman society? Unquestionably, marriages in Paul's time were male-dominated. Did Paul see this as the universal nature of things, or as the customary arrangement, like the understanding of servers and customers in a restaurant?

This is not the place to untangle such a question, even if I could. For women in Paul's original audience, perhaps the distinction made no difference. Either way, they were asked to submit to their husbands.

However, Paul's directions to husbands and wives reveal something important about submission. He might very easily have told husbands to take control of their wives, asserting male authority by force if necessary. That would have been a very natural way for men to see marriage in those days. Paul could have framed his instructions around male power. In fact, that is how his advice has often been applied. Male superiority and male domination have been read into the text.

That is not at all how Paul writes. Paul frames his instructions around love and respect. He instructs husbands to *love* their wives. He tells wives to choose submission in the same way they relate to the Lord: willingly. Paul doesn't threaten. He appeals. He evidently regards wives as holding power too—the power to choose. That is why his marital advice fits perfectly with the preceding verse, which tells everyone to "submit to one another out of reverence for Christ" (Ephesians 5:21).

Submission applies to all of us, wherever we are called to fit into the universe. We all must submit. Different power arrangements might be theoretically possible, but we are asked to fit in. Such a choice need not involve a loss of dignity. Rather, we demonstrate maturity and wisdom when we submit.

People who lack the maturity to submit gain lots of trouble. In school they get kicked out of class. They get lectured at work and avoided in church. Even their family members find them difficult. They can't work on a team because they aren't humble enough to fit in.

There's a time and a place for rebellion. We want people to stand up for what is right against the power structure. Even rebels, though, have to know proper submission, or they'll always be lonely rebels, without allies.

TRAINING FOR SUBMISSION

My friend Marlene writes, "I just wish that I had caught on to submission when I was younger. I think I relished my independent spirit too much. I hated youth choir specifically because I was under the control of the choir director ('imprisoned' was my word) and had to pay attention to details. I didn't learn tennis because of the specific rules of how to play. Now I regret it and see that freedom comes from submission. One important question is how to get kids to see the value of submission—especially when the child is strong-willed."

The answer, I think, lies in family culture. I find it hard to list family activities that particularly teach submission, because they all do. School, sports, work, family events, friendships—all give opportunities.

You learn submission in three great areas. First is submission to the task—following through on commitments, giving your best effort. You don't have to like the job, but you submit to its requirements. Personally, I remember finishing the dishes—including the burned-on pot.

Second, submission involves obedience to authority and respect for authority. You not only do what the teacher requires, you show respect. Attitude goes with action. I remember my father's unwavering demand that I speak respectfully to my mother.

Third, you submit to disappointment and loss. Have to wait in line because there are too few clerks for the rush? Can't get the class you wanted this semester? Accept frustration and disappointment without grumbling.

I remember learning this lesson on a camping trip. We ended up in a location I didn't like. After I had grumbled and complained for a while, my mother spoke to me firmly. "I've learned in life," she said, "not to compare." Submission meant shrugging off the burden of disappointment and looking for the best in a situation. I never forgot that lesson.

Ultimately you submit to God. He is in control of the universe. You may not like the way things work out, yet you humble yourself under God, trusting that in good time he will lift you up (James 4:10; 1 Peter 5:6).

OBEYING PARENTS

The first authority any of us meets is Mom or Dad, and we first learn submission with them. The Bible tells children to obey their parents. This is situational submission. But the Bible tells adults to honor their parents, which is different from obedience. (*Honor* is in the Ten Commandments. *Obedience* isn't.) Children obey for practical reasons. Parents are experienced and children are not. We do not want children controlling credit cards or deciding whether to do homework until they have enough experience to make such judgments for themselves.

Parents are imperfect authorities, as children find out very early. Parents make mistakes. The same comment applies to teachers, bosses, coaches, waiters and every other individual who holds temporary authority in our lives. Yet parents have been placed in control. From early experiences with their parents, children learn this core value of submission. They will use it throughout life.

Everybody will benefit if parents start these lessons early. Some parents make the mistake of thinking little kids are cute when they disobey. Perhaps the comparison is unsavory, but pet owners make the same mistake when they let puppies bite. Dog parents don't put up with misbehavior for a second, and human parents shouldn't either. Correction need not be harsh, only firm. You can do it in whatever style you find comfortable—but do it. If you don't create a family culture that expects obedience to parents, you will make learning these lessons much harder later on in life. And you will do your children no favor.

Some families have a culture of obedience like the Marine Corps. They expect absolute, unquestioning obedience, with no show of resistance or dislike. They treat like treason any questioning of parental authority.

At the other extreme, some families adopt very flexible parenting, encouraging plenty of input and dialogue, and avoiding as much as possible the apparent harshness of parental decrees.

Popie and I have taken the second way. We're not comfortable with the role of authoritarian parent. I have to admit, though, that the bottom line remains pretty much the same. Parents make decisions on behalf of their children. Even if they let children make some choices for themselves (what to eat, how to spend free time, whom to pursue as friends) they are conscious of holding ultimate authority. Just because I don't make a point of my authority doesn't make me any less the authority. In fact, a boss or a commanding general or a parent who feels securely in control may hold the reins looser than one who feels uncertain of his or her command.

RESPECTING ELDERS

Submission involves attitude as well as action. We really don't want to produce people who only submit grudgingly and grumpily.

Submission doesn't require that you're always delighted to obey. You may disagree with the decision at hand, but you continue to believe that the authority isn't arbitrary, and you treat it with respect. In military terms, you salute the uniform.

One way children learn the attitude of submission is through respecting their elders. Some families emphasize this respect by having children address adults as "Mr. Smith" or "Mrs. Albert." Other traditions have children stand whenever adults enter the room. The old saying "Children should be seen and not heard" represents yet another way of teaching respect for elders. Many societies around the world still practice it.

Some will find these approaches old-fashioned and excessively formal. All is not lost. Simple good manners with elders, such as introducing friends to them, or shaking hands when meeting, will go some distance to emphasize respect. How would you like your little son to behave if someday the high school principal came to the door? Teach him to respond to his grandparents in the same way now.

The way children learn to behave with grandparents, aunts, uncles and family friends will influence the way they treat authority figures for the rest of their lives.

FAMILY ACTIVITIES

Almost any family activity calls on family members—parents included—
to submit to the project. For example, a card game involves following the
rules, taking turns and not pouting when you lose. As parents take their
turn like everybody else, children see submission modeled. They can see
the same factors at play in a family picnic, in choosing a movie to watch
at home or in celebrating Mother's Day. Everybody has to work together.
Each person must submit to the joint project.

My friend Marlene writes, "As missionaries we often had other folks
stay in our home. We would welcome them together, ask questions and
listen together. Our daughter Annelies was not the center of the attention; the guest was. She learned to care for others that way. She caught
on quickly, too, that being a compliant and pleasant young woman
brought its own rewards." The more parents involve children in family
activities, the more opportunities they will have to teach the art of fitting
in. We make a mistake when we let kids operate in a parallel universe,
unconnected to adults. We do children no favor if we make them the
center of attention at all times.

COMPETITION

Most American families get involved in some kind of team sports or competition. Competition offers multiple opportunities to learn submission.

First of all, there's teamwork. Consider soccer. Good players work
hard at moving without the ball. They study the movements of their
teammates, particularly the player who is dribbling the ball. They respond creatively to the teammate's initiative. That's submission.

When kids first start to play, they all converge on the ball. Coaches
have to teach them to spread out and anticipate their teammates' moves.
The success of the team depends on each player finding his or her proper
role in response to others. Players have to move back and forth between
initiative and support. When players all try to star, there's usually a negative result for the team.

Every sport offers such lessons. Families can underline the values of
teamwork as they review games, discussing what went wrong and what

went right. And when they see a child showboating or hogging, they can point out how bad that is for the team. Some children need a lot of correction before they get the idea of teamwork.

Coaches need (and appreciate) players who follow directions, especially with an enthusiastic attitude. Coaches don't appreciate players who groan over the choice of drills in practice, who complain that they're not playing the position they want, who second guess the coach's strategy. Parents who want their children to learn the core value of submission will emphasize the coach's authority. They won't undermine it by sympathizing with their children about "unfair" decisions the coach made. They may, in fact, consider the coach unfair themselves. But they do better to respond this way: "Well, she's the coach. You and I may disagree with her decisions, but the bottom line is that she has the job of making decisions for your team. Your job is to do the very best you can to carry out those decisions."

Of course, you can suggest that your child raise his or her questions with the coach in private, with appropriate respect. That is part of submission too: learning how to express individual thoughts while still supporting the person in authority.

Finally, all competition teaches submission to failure. If you play long enough, you'll probably experience as many losses as wins. Disappointment is chronic, since we can't help dreaming of the undefeated season. This is the best thing about competition. It trains you for one of the hardest aspects of life—failure.

If athletics is a spiritual development course, the most advanced learners tend to be the mediocre athletes. The real sports superstars may not grapple with disappointment at all. They're too successful. They don't know failure. As a result, they're at risk for babyish, spoiled character. Read the sports page and you often glimpse why winning isn't everything.

You can, of course, get angry at defeat, make excuses, blame teammates or officials and stomp around in a huff. None of this will help. You have to come to terms with the fact that you lost. Submitting doesn't mean accepting permanent failure or thinking less of yourself. It means you accept disappointment, you look the results in the eye—and you move on. Perhaps you dedicate yourself to working harder. Perhaps you conclude that you would be better off playing another game. Most likely, you shrug it off with the realization that, if you did your best, you did all that you could do. And you got to play the game!

Almost universally, parents identify with their children as they compete in sports or other competitive endeavors. They enjoy the thrills with them. They suffer when their children lose. Parents have to submit too. Sometimes you want to jump all over the referees, complain about the coaches, even yell ugly things at the opponents. Being a parent, though, you must show your children how an adult should respond. That means submission. If you can't do it, your children never will.

Jobs

Whether a young worker does chores around the house, mows the neighbor's lawn or starts his first full-time job, he or she is bound to get lessons in submission. Work is difficult, which is why you get paid. Young people don't usually get the most interesting jobs. Submission means sticking to it, not complaining and not loafing.

Then there's humility before the boss—the willingness to take orders cheerfully and work the way you're told. A lot of young people are very quick to disrespect the boss. And, of course, some bosses are very poor at what they do. Nevertheless, you can hardly learn a more useful lesson in life than submission to the boss, in attitude and action.

Finally there is submission to your status. I remember very well that when I started out as a magazine editor, I had little respect for those who had been editing magazines for years. I was impatient with my elders, sure of my opinions. I think that is typical of young people. They expect to be promoted long before their elders even notice their existence. Sometimes the young people are right: they *could* do it better. Sometimes they are just impatient, unaware of how much they don't know. Either way, whether right or wrong, they will have to wait and learn submission.

Employers look for these forms of submission. Yes, they need employees trained in the latest software, who communicate well and have good mathematical skills. Even more, though, they need workers with the attitudes and values to perform as good team members, to work alongside others, to take direction.

CHURCH

The Bible treats the fellowship of believers as essential. Think of the metaphor of the body of Christ, which Paul introduced in 1 Corinthians 12. An individual Christian, detached from other believers, is like a hand without an arm. He or she is useless!

Yet many Christians do wander away from regular church involvement. To put it simply, they haven't learned to submit. They don't submit to the ordinary faults and flaws, the dullness and blindness of any human organization. They don't submit to the church's pastors and elders. Because the church isn't perfect, they can't stand to stick with it.

Submission at church starts with the example of parents. They find ways to get along with leaders and fellow members. They're respectful. They don't eat roast pastor for Sunday lunch. They encourage their children to treat church with appreciation and respect—and to find ways to fit in.

Submission can be learned in almost any activity more demanding than a video game. Always there is teamwork. Always there are difficult tasks to stick to. Always there are bosses and coaches to heed and respect. Always disappointments come that one must accept.

Family culture teaches submission not by adding activities to the schedule but by watching carefully for lessons in the activities of the day. The style of instruction will vary from family to family, and it must be reinforced hundreds of times, perhaps thousands, in example as well as precept. Even for the most mature of adults, submission requires an emotional struggle. It comes as humility gains the upper hand in your heart, and as trust in God covers over your fears and dislikes.

How can any child learn this, which is so difficult for adults? Only by growing in a family that practices it, and works at it, and speaks of it. To speak plainly, a great many families don't. Those who do, who make humility and submission habits of mind and heart, pass on a core value of the greatest significance.

11

BOUNDARIES

Developing a Sense of Self

"You shall not steal." EXODUS 20:15

*"Do not move an ancient boundary stone
or encroach on the fields of the fatherless,
for their Defender is strong;
he will take up their case against you."*
PROVERBS 23:10-11

*"Do you not know that your body is a temple of the Holy Spirit,
who is in you, whom you have received from God? . . .
Therefore honor God with your body."* 1 CORINTHIANS 6:19-20

"Above all else, guard your heart, for it is the wellspring of life."
PROVERBS 4:23

Here is a mother-in-law joke, taken from a website devoted to the genre:

> Every time Bill brought home a girl to meet his mother, his mother
> didn't like her. Finally he started searching until he found a girl
> who not only looked like his mother and acted like his mother, she
> even sounded like his mother. So he brought her home to dinner
> one night—and his father didn't like her.

The overbearing mother-in-law is a classic of folk mythology. Everybody knows this woman, even if they've never met her. She feels free to offer her daughter-in-law plentiful advice on how to cook her son's breakfast, iron his shirts and even clean his house. She drops by uninvited and stays too long. She asks nosy questions about why they haven't started a family. Essentially, she acts as though her life and her son's life are one and the same. They ought to be two circles that touch each other, but in her understanding his circle fits inside her circle. She has never figured out that the doctor cut the umbilical cord.

The modern terminology for this very ancient reality is *boundaries*. The mother has a poor sense of boundaries. She doesn't understand that her life ends where her son's begins. Instead she tries to live her life through his.

Her behavior can be very well meant. I have an aunt who, according to family legend, had to put her foot down lest her in-laws come along on her honeymoon. They loved their son, they wanted to welcome their new daughter into the family, and they thought it would be wonderful to share that precious time together. Fortunately, my aunt knew her limits.

A CORE VALUE

I don't mean to pick on mothers-in-law. (Mine is wonderful.) Consider the micromanaging boss or the nosy neighbor, two other stock characters who don't recognize boundaries. Adults know plenty of such people. However, they don't usually think of preparing their children to face them. They don't think about the universal significance of the issue. They should. Boundaries are a core value.

Take the case of a girl whose sense of boundaries is so weak and ill-defined that other people's lives swamp her own. When somebody makes a mean comment to her, she takes it completely to heart. The girl who sits next to her in class tells her she's worthless? Presto change-o, she becomes worthless. She doesn't have a boundary that keeps others' comments as "just your opinion." Their views go straight through her.

Because of this, her self-esteem goes up and down like a weather balloon. Sometimes she seems so full of herself she's almost bragging, but the confidence is hollow. If someone steals her favorite pen, she can't demand it back—she just feels blue and helpless. And when she gets old enough to go out with boys, she will get used just about any way a boy wants, because she doesn't know how to say no. She thinks her life depends on a boy liking her.

Very often, the girl grows up to become the mother-in-law. Lacking a sense of her own boundaries, she doesn't recognize them in anybody else. And then she helps create a son who himself lacks a sense of boundaries—perhaps one of those raging, self-absorbed boys who wreak havoc in class and on the playground. The cycle can go on endlessly.

THE ANCIENT BOUNDARY STONES

The human race has always produced people who lack boundaries, but the problem grows particularly acute under chaotic social situations. For example, looting and rape—boundary crimes—grow common in times of war. A soldier who has never stolen in his life will decide to "lift" something from a house, because he's lost any sense that it belongs to somebody. Soldiers will rape indiscriminately, because in the haze of war they can't see that they are dealing with human beings.

Similarly, people who are raised in chaotic family situations often lose a clear sense of boundaries. They get abused, or abuse others, apparently without any sense that lines are violated. Tremendous emotional confusion follows. That's at least one reason why divorce leads to so many problems for the next generation. The breakup of a family is one of the worst kinds of social chaos. Many families feature a shifting cast of mothers and fathers and brothers and sisters. Life becomes unpredictable, and it often leaves children with a weakened sense of themselves and others. They react in contradictory ways: perhaps by trying to exert control over everything, perhaps by seeking someone (or some group) strong enough to provide them with an identity. They are desperately trying to figure out who they are and how they fit in with other people.

THE ENTITLED SELF

Perhaps because we live in an era of such rapid change, Westerners today are very attuned to boundaries. They put great emphasis on the entitled self with highly defended boundaries. Many stress their rights. They urge each other, "Don't let people take advantage of you." The way some people talk, healthy boundaries don't leave much space for service or self-sacrifice.

For this reason I have some ambivalence in discussing boundaries as a core value. I think boundaries are often misapplied. Today's entitled self is not a sign of healthy boundaries. More likely it reflects uncertainty in chaotic times. If people defend their rights with disproportionate ferocity, it may be because they feel very unsure of themselves.

People with a strong sense of self don't have to talk about themselves and their prerogatives. They know their own business and aren't worried that anybody will encroach on it. They can give freely to others without losing track of their own rights and responsibilities. Good boundaries free us for service. How can you give yourself to others unless you know who you are?

Family culture can teach children that they are valuable as individuals, that each one of us has God-given rights and responsibilities that no one can take away. Family culture can create the regular, calm environment where people gain a sense of self. Fundamentally, I am me and you are you. God has put each one of us in charge of his or her own life and body. For many families, these are matters of common sense and simple respect.

ZONES OF PRIVACY

Every individual needs privacy and has a right to privacy. This need will increase as a child grows older. Teenagers need a lot more privacy than toddlers because their lives are far larger and more individuated.

Parents can become so intent on their children's welfare that they invade their private thoughts and private lives. That is not God's way. He urges us, he helps us, but he does not invade us. He knows that while he could coerce obedience, he cannot coerce faith. He lets us lead our own lives. He even lets us ignore him. He is willing to let us live as individuals who sometimes choose what's wrong.

Healthy families recognize that while they must be involved in children's choices, there are limits to their involvement. They will set the limits in different places, depending on the family. In some families you don't have to tell what you're thinking. In some, you don't have to tell what girl or boy you're attracted to. In some, you don't have to tell where you're going or what you're planning, at least under certain circumstances. ("As long as you're in by midnight," some parents say to their teenagers, "I trust you to act responsibly.") In some families, you don't have to tell where you spend your money.

There's bound to be some tugging and pushing on these issues, at least when teenagers are involved. Teenagers experiment with boundaries. One minute they will push boundaries out to infinity—there's *no* limit to the privacy they demand—and the next they may want you to know everything.

Wise parents recognize that there are limits to what they can know and should know about their children's lives. They don't badger their children to disclose information that really is personal.

Many people write down their most intense reflective thoughts in a diary. Others reveal their inner selves in correspondence—letters, e-mails or instant messages—to a best friend. These can and often do become battlegrounds of privacy. Parents have an intense desire to know what goes on in their children's heads. Yet fostering an understanding of boundaries means setting limits on your curiosity.

For many families, diaries and personal correspondence are explicitly off limits. Family members pledge to restrain themselves from digging into them.

The problem with this pledge comes when parents are genuinely worried about dangerous behavior. For example: Is my child contemplating suicide? Is my child using drugs? sexually involved? trading pornography? In my judgment, a parent's responsibilities sometimes outweigh the importance of privacy.

Unfortunately, some parents don't have good judgment. They're endlessly suspicious, they're always probing, and a child who wants privacy for his or her thoughts feels that it's impossible to get. (Such children often can't wait to grow up and leave home.)

Sometimes a compromise can be found through a heart-to-heart talk. In it, the parents say explicitly that they don't want to pry into private details of life, but that they must first feel confidence that no destructive behavior is going on. That gives children a fair warning: if they want privacy, they have to be forthcoming with the information their parents need in order to be good parents.

PRIVATE POSSESSIONS

I know a family that lives in a very small apartment. Each member of the family has his or her possessions—clothes, toys, games, music—and they absolutely don't exchange or borrow anything from each other. They feel that those distinctions of ownership need careful preservation, given how tightly they live. Other families feel free to borrow clothes, music, whatever, so long as they ask permission. Whatever the family style, private possessions help establish the concept of boundaries. Children grow up with control over certain items—not of the whole world, but of a limited arena that they can really, truly call "mine."

PRIVATE SPACE

Many American families can afford to give each family member his or her own room. In families where children share bedrooms, each one may have a designated area that's "all hers." A bed, bookcase or closet can be a child's private space. Sometimes families designate a space in the garden where anyone can go if they don't want interruptions.

The concept of private space helps to establish boundaries. As with possessions, a child has a sense of control over an area where he or she can live according to his or her taste.

PRIVATE PARTS

As part of sex education, I believe every child should be taught at a very young age that they have "private parts" that no one but them may see or touch. Exceptions will, of course, be explained: the doctor, for example, or parents who need to inspect or treat a rash or a lump. In general children can learn from the age of three or four that God has given them a body that belongs to them alone. They should learn that no one—not friends, not cousins, not grandparents, not teachers—has any business seeing or touching certain precious and private parts. This need not be taught so as to inculcate fear. It should be taught so as to inculcate pride, self-respect and a sense of integrity. This is my body, and it has been given to me.

Modesty, of course, is very cultural. People in other parts of the world may have a wildly different sense of modesty than do Americans. Regardless of the standard, the point is that modesty is not to be tossed away as outmoded Victorianism. People need to understand that their bodies are not a public commodity. It's right and proper to shield them from public view.

As I have corresponded with thousands of young people about love and sex, I have found that many never were taught a sense of sexual privacy. They feel that they have to answer any question asked of them, such as "Are you a virgin?" or "How far did you go with her?" I try to inform them that the proper answer to any such question is, "None of your business."

They may also feel an obligation to "give out" as payment for a nice evening or an expensive dinner. They may feel that if they "love" somebody, they are obligated to share their bodies. Such young people desperately need the core value of boundaries. They don't have to explain or justify a decision not to have sex, or even a decision not to kiss.

STEALING

One of the Ten Commandments, "You shall not steal," is sometimes cited by economic conservatives as a biblical defense of private property. It is that, but not because God wanted to defend capitalism. Rather, it has to do with preserving the boundaries of human life. This is particularly clear if you think of the context in which the Ten Commandments were given. For a nomadic, shepherding people, homes, clothing and flocks become an extension of who they are. A world that doesn't outlaw stealing—that allows anyone to take what they will, by force or by custom—allows very little space for individuals to be themselves and to develop independent lives.

Children will always push the boundaries, and that may include trying a little pilfering to get what they want. Many families treat theft
lightly, because not much money was taken and "he didn't intend any
harm." That is a mistake. The monetary value may be very small when a
child snatches a candy bar from the grocery store (or from her brother),
but the values are very large. When we treat theft seriously we're teaching the value of boundaries.

MANNERS

Manners are always changing, which is not necessarily a sign of the end
of civilization. Whether or not men open doors for women, whether or
not boys take off their baseball caps when they enter a room, whether or
not girls call boys on the telephone, are matters of custom, not morality.

Manners change, but their overall purpose does not. Manners are sig-
nals meant to convey respect for other people, and to create an orderly,
"boundaried" sense of social space. We teach manners to children so that
they will learn how to live respectfully with others.

Some manners are quite directly involved with boundaries. For example, in conversation we apply the basic rule of not interrupting others. Few things are more personal than speech, and the rule insures that
each person—even a small child—will get a moment of uninterrupted
control to say what she wants to say, in the manner in which she wants
to say it. Then, of course, she will have to give the same opportunity to
someone else.

Keeping this rule can sometimes be difficult—for example, when a
child wants to tell a parent something, but the parent is deeply involved
in an adult conversation. I like the idea that the child put a hand on the
parent and keep it there until he is recognized. It's not a bad suggestion
between adult family members, either.

ALLOWANCE

A weekly or monthly allowance gives a child experience with personal
control. The main point is education. Allowances teach the habit of making very personal decisions about something very important: money.

Children experience a region of their own jurisdiction in the realm of possessions. And yet there is a limit. The child's autonomy is not boundless. He or she learns that when all the money is spent, there's no more.

The amount of allowance, and what it is supposed to cover, can vary widely from family to family. I don't think there is any right or wrong to this. It depends a lot on the personality and interests of the child. A child who cares greatly about clothes, for instance, can receive a regular clothing allowance. Other children, lacking an interest in what they wear, will be in rags before they spend any of their own money on clothes; they may be better off with clothes purchased by their parents.

CHORES

An allowance gives children a sense of control; chores give them a sense of obligation and competence.

When I was very small I was given the job of making juice in the morning. I can remember it very clearly, right down to the tiniest detail. I learned how to measure very carefully three cans of water, and how to stir thoroughly until all the frozen concentrate was absorbed. My mother always made a point of complimenting me on a job well done. She said that I did such a good job that the orange juice tasted better when I made it.

I was very proud of my orange juice, and I concentrated hard on doing my best. At that age it was probably the only contribution I made to the family, but I gained satisfaction that I could do it well. That is how chores contribute to a sense of boundaries and personal worth.

JOBS

As with chores, jobs build a sense of accountability. They teach young people that there is a sharp distinction between their life and everybody else's. You have your own social security number, you do your own work, and you get your own reward.

RITES OF PASSAGE

Every culture has certain ceremonial passages to mark movement between stages of life. In Jewish culture, the bar mitzvah or bat mitzvah marks the age of accountability. A boy or a girl takes on, symbolically, the privileges and responsibilities of adulthood.

In many African tribes, rites of circumcision mark a similar transformation. A Kenyan psychiatrist once told me that only in religious conversion had he seen such dramatic personality changes as those marked by circumcision in his tribe.

In America we also have certain rites of passage. One is the driver's license. Another is high school graduation. Some families make a big deal out of these. Doing so in the right way can put a punctuation mark on a sudden leap in personal responsibility and control.

A driver's license gives a teenager more control over where they will go and whom they will go with. It's worth celebrating! Some families underline the responsibility by insisting that teenagers pay for a year of car insurance. They may also add some driving chores, like taking younger children to and from school.

Graduating from high school is, similarly, a big deal. Some families throw a big party or give significant gifts. After graduation, you're assumed to be capable of independence. Many families stop insisting on a curfew. In essence, the message is that you're an adult.

Some churches make a great deal of first communion, or church membership, or adult baptism. These emphasize the growth of a person within Christ's kingdom. The individual has reached an age of personal maturity and responsibility before God and in the church. It deserves marking!

In all these rites of passage, you want to bring affirmation to the person who is gaining new privileges and responsibilities. The young person's freedoms within the boundaries of self grow clearer and stronger. They become more of themselves! A family can mark such an event by throwing a party, by making strict requirements, or just by talking about it. For the person who is growing up, the notice itself can help create a sense of personal integrity.

FAMILIES ARE CRUCIAL

An orderly family environment gives children a sense that life is predictable, so they can exert some control over it. A respectful environment teaches children that they have individual dignity and *deserve* to have some control. Parents need to provide limits, so that children will know their autonomy is not endless, and privacy, so that children will feel freedom to be themselves and to dream their own dreams. Children also need responsibilities, so they can learn how it feels to exert control over a defined area.

Boundaries are learned through very common aspects of family life: chores, allowances, manners, possessions. At their basis is an attitude, one modeled by God himself in all our dealings with him. He gives us strict limits in what we can do and how far we can go, but yet he respects our freedom to the uttermost. He has given us our lives, and they are ours to use. Parents must teach the same grave responsibility to their children.

12

JOY AND THANKSGIVING
Learning a Happy Heart

"Be joyful in hope." ROMANS 12:12

"Rejoice in the Lord always." PHILIPPIANS 4:4

*"I have not stopped giving thanks for you,
remembering you in my prayers."* EPHESIANS 1:16

"Since we are receiving a kingdom . . . let us be thankful."
HEBREWS 12:28

*"Let us continually offer to God a sacrifice of praise—
the fruit of lips that confess his name."* HEBREWS 13:15

It may seem strange to speak of joy as a core value. We tend to think of joy as spontaneous and untrained, while core values are bedrock, serious and solemn. How can you tame joy into a habit?

This reminds me of a story my mother tells. When she was a little girl, her father was trying to take a photo of his daughters. My mother and her sister were acting out, not cooperating. Their father grew angrier and angrier as he tried vainly to get the pose he wanted. His daughters, in turn, grew more and more impatient and upset. Finally, in exasperation, my grandfather shouted at them, "Smile or I'll spank you!" The resulting expressions, caught on film, were very imperfect representations of joy.

Joy is not easily commanded. Yet the Scriptures are filled with commands to rejoice, to be joyful, to give thanks, to praise. Evidently we are supposed to experience joy whether we feel like it or not. Joy is a matter of choice.

We all know people who are consistently joy-filled, who see the bright side, who lift our spirits, who appear thankful no matter what the weather. (We also know people who have a talent for seeing the hole in the donut.) Were they born sunny? If you ask them, they'll tell you no. They are invariably conscious of choosing their responses. They work at being positive.

I'm not saying they get all the credit. If you trace back the habit of joy, you'll usually find a parent who was similarly positive. Most joyful people were raised in a home where they saw joy modeled daily. Joy is part of their inherited family culture, which they choose to carry on.

Joy comes with more difficulty for others. Take me as an example. By nature I'm a sober personality. I don't gush, and I never have. More than a few of my friends have mistaken my somber expression for a critical spirit, which I don't think I particularly possess. What I do have is a repressed personality. I'm not always in touch with my feelings, and when I am, I'm usually a day late. I start laughing at a joke after everybody else has gone home from the party. I start weeping the day after the funeral.

People like me don't come naturally to joy and thanksgiving. The instinct may be in our souls, but it is deeply buried. And yet we too are commanded to rejoice. The truth is, we *need* to rejoice. Joy releases our better selves. It relaxes our spirits. We aren't healthy people unless we learn to rejoice.

However, we have to do it in a way that suits us. And here is a very basic and important point: you don't have to be perky in order to be joyful. Joy can be quiet or loud, Pentecostal or Presbyterian. It can be done in the style of a Florida State cheerleader or in the calm manner of a college professor. There are many approaches to joy. That's where family culture helps. It's flexible. By developing a family culture of joy, one that suits your family's personalities, you can greatly help your children to become comfortable in their own skins.

For myself, I spent many years feeling uncomfortable around others' more exuberant expressions of joy. For example, charismatic praise services made me extremely anxious, because I wanted to join in wholeheartedly and yet felt too inhibited. Eventually I recognized that there are lots of ways to praise God, that culture has a large role in what we feel comfortable with, and that it's okay to be quiet in a noisy assembly.

We need not express joy in any particular way, but we need to find some way. There is a form of godliness that has nothing merry in it, but that is not God's preference. I like Psalm 104, which celebrates the great diversity of creation, and I particularly like verse 26:

> There the ships go to and fro
>   and the leviathan, which you formed to frolic there.

The contrast between the busy, businesslike ships doing humanity's work and the frolicking whale, utterly indifferent to us, is a useful reminder not to take ourselves too seriously. The leviathan doesn't! Sometimes the best way to respond to life is to slap your tail on the water.

Life may not always be fun, but every moment of every day offers reasons to give thanks. Why? Because "the earth is the LORD's, and everything in it" (Psalm 24:1). Look around you, and you will see reasons for joy.

We want to be people who know the value of joy and practice it every day of their lives. We want to be people who are habitually thankful. Family culture can train that kind of people.

SAYING THANKS

For most American families, thankfulness starts with teaching children to say thank you. I'm so committed to this that I'm tempted to say it's required. The truth is, though, that thanks is deeply cultural. There are places in the world where people never say thank you. It's just not one of their cultural practices. It doesn't mean they don't know joy and thanksgiving.

That said, the habit of saying thank you is a very basic and powerful tool. Teaching it to children requires massive commitment on the part of parents, because at a very young age you have to begin at least a million repetitions of what sometimes seems silly and pointless. "Say thank you!" "Timmy, what do you say to your aunt?" Kids do not learn this by instinct, nor do they pick it up never to forget it the way they do with riding a bike or tying shoes. They have to be reminded and reinforced, and the words must sometimes be insisted on for at least a decade.

Of course, the result is purely a societal convention, words that can be used by people who are not really thankful at all, who merely possess good manners. Saying thanks is just a beginning. It can, however, shape us in preparation for the next step. Once a child has been taught to say thank you, he or she is primed for the realization that thanksgiving is always required.

GRACE

Many families say a prayer before they eat. Some vary the practice and say a prayer after the meal, or before dessert. Some use a rote prayer; some like to sing. Saying grace can be rotated around the family, so everybody gets a turn. Prayer can be long, making a kind of brief family devotions, or prayer can be very short: "Thank you, God, for this food." In my extended family we usually say grace at family reunions by singing the doxology: "Praise God from whom all blessings flow." Because singing is part of our family culture, and nearly everyone can sing harmony, we produce some wonderful and memorable sounds!

Any of these ways of saying grace makes a powerful and repeated statement: we depend on God for daily existence. We consider it essential to pause, recognize his gifts and thank him for them. Like saying thank you to each other, even for the most ordinary help, grace at the table reinforces the understanding that we owe God thanks constantly, almost unthinkingly.

"Unthinkingly," of course, can be a problem. Like anything we do repeatedly, grace can lose its meaning and be spun out of our mouths as rote phrases. It takes work to keep grace meaningful. Sometimes it helps to change the way we do it—singing instead of speaking, reading a prayer, lighting a candle, praying after the meal rather than before. Change can draw attention to the prayer and encourage renewed thoughtfulness.

CELEBRATIONS

There's a reason why virtually every culture has its special celebratory holidays. It's in our makeup as human beings to set aside certain times and days to celebrate. Spaniards erect huge papier-mâché statues and burn them. They also run through the streets in front of dangerous bulls. Americans blow off fireworks and eat large birds. Whatever we do in celebration, it's meant to be extravagant fun. Celebration trains us to let go, to enjoy existence, to experience joy.

Here's the main problem: celebrations take time. Busy people don't always take the time required. Even if it's a national holiday, like the Fourth of July, they want to accomplish so much that they don't relax and celebrate. They just don't see the point. Holidays don't have a utilitarian purpose. There is no lesson to be learned from watching a parade. Which is part of the point. The point is there is no point. Joy is not about accomplishing something.

Families cultivate the habit of joy by making the most of holidays— or by inventing their own special celebrations. Holiday traditions definitely stick! Ask any senior citizen to describe their childhood family celebrations, and you will find that the memories have never faded.

CHRISTMAS AND EASTER

Not all holiday traditions are created equal. The great church celebrations of Christmas and Easter provide a lot of room for family joy, and they remember events that are worthy of the most joyful celebration. Some families decorate the house in special ways. They bring out special music and have special treats. (Holiday cookies stay with you in more ways than one.) They have a tradition of special family gatherings, sometimes complete with a musical talent show or a family worship service. They attend special services (midnight on Christmas Eve, sunrise at Easter).

Some people complain about extravagant materialism, claiming that there's no Christ in Christmas. I think though, that we can take pleasure in the good cheer and family joy we share with our neighbors of all faiths and none. Then we go beyond, adding the deeper celebration of God's coming to earth.

The same with Easter. I was raised to be suspicious of the Easter bunny. What did it have to do with the risen Jesus? My wife, on the other hand, grew up with a tradition of baby chicks dyed in bright colors. I don't think it did her any harm. It certainly made her love Easter! Of course, if the Easter bunny were the main text of Easter, that would be a serious problem. But I don't believe the Easter bunny gives our risen Lord any real competition. If your Easter includes both, the real Jesus need not be cheated.

BIRTHDAYS

Some families don't just celebrate birthdays, they celebrate birth weeks. The celebration of a person's birth (and life) is anticipated and enjoyed in multiple celebrations. Birthdays can be extravagant fun!

With or without words, though, birthdays give us opportunity to take joy in the individual. And note: everybody has a birthday, so everybody gets celebrated. Implied in the celebration is this fact: every single individual on the face of the earth is someone to thank God for.

INVENT YOUR OWN CELEBRATION

What are the important days in your family history? The day you moved into your house? The day you got your citizenship papers? The day you started your job? The day you gave away the car seat? Mark them! Celebrate them! Give thanks for them! Find creative ways to add joy and celebration to your family life.

A friend of mine, Steve, told me how their family celebrated the day of the last diaper. They all piled in the car and took the old diaper pail to the dump. With great joy Steve threw the smelly thing as far into the landfill as he could. I don't know what the children thought, but for Steve and Leslie, that was a joyful day!

FUN NIGHTS

Some people may want to sharply distinguish between joy and fun. My opinion, however, is that the two are hard to separate. Emotions just don't differentiate themselves that distinctively.

One family I know, when the kids were small, celebrated something called Pajama Night. These funfests always came without warning. When the kids were in bed and drifting off to sleep, the lights would flash on and off, loud music would come on the stereo, and the whole family would pile out of bed and into the minivan. They would then drive around the neighborhood in their pajamas, listening to loud music on the car stereo.

That was silly, cheap fun. And they loved it. Other families have regular game nights, when they eat popcorn and play board games together.

In many families I know, parents and children have wrestling matches on a regular basis—arm wrestling, Tag Team wrestling, whatever their circumstances and preferences allow. In other families dancing prevails—the music goes up loud and everybody who dares cuts a rug on the living room floor. (I myself have been trying for years to convince my kids that the Twist is a really cool dance. They mock me, of course.)

Which reminds me, a step in child development that I particularly enjoy (and have never seen noted in a book) is when children become genuinely funny in making fun of their parents. Parents can look forward to this day and celebrate it.

Fun is not exactly joy and thanksgiving. On the other hand, it is not terribly far from joy and thanksgiving. Through such traditions, families teach each other how to lighten up, let go, act a little less serious. We want to be people who know how to laugh!

MUSIC

God gave us music in order to help us express our feelings. There is nothing quite like it for joy and praise, which explains why worship services ordinarily have music at their heart.

Some families bring music into the heart of their family. This is a very different business from sending the kids to music lessons or having them join the choir at school. It means finding ways to do music together.

I know one family that indulged the father's taste in rock music by starting their own band. They even recorded their own CD. It was purely an amateur effort, but they had a wonderful time doing it.

In another family, five sisters sang close harmony while they did the dishes each night. In another, the parents and kids get out their instruments at Christmas and play carols. In another, Christmas family celebrations always involve caroling together, sometimes for the neighbors, sometimes at a nursing home

Families that lack musicians can find joy in listening together—attending special concerts or even listening to CDs together at home. Music teaches us how to rejoice, to put our hearts into it. And families, because they are close and small and safe, make wonderful training schools for such music.

PRAISE

I'm convinced that every aspect of our relationship to God has a human correlation. We learn to be thankful to God by learning to thank Aunt Mary for the sweater. We learn how to celebrate God's greatness as we experience fireworks on the Fourth of July.

It's the same with praise. If you are a grumpy person who never has an affirming word to say to your children, then I very much doubt that your praise to God can be honest and true.

Praise can become part of your family culture, if you work at it. My wife is an expert at affirmation—the most gifted and consistent person I've ever met at skillfully praising people. She's not content to leave it there, though. She expects the rest of the family to join in. She does it by asking questions— "Aren't you impressed by what your brother did at the concert?"—and by insisting on rituals such as birthday affirmations. She often puts us on the spot to say a word of encouragement or praise to another family member or to a guest. The experience can be embarrassing, but it teaches good lessons.

These same spontaneous practices cross over to praising God. For example, it's a simple practice to add to your grace before meals some thanks for the events of the day. Even more memorable is to pause to pray whenever significant, life-changing events occur. Someone gets into the college they hoped to? Stop and gather the family to pray. You hear that a beloved grandfather has died? Take time immediately to thank

God for his life. A vacation trip takes you to the top of the world, where you can see for a hundred glorious miles? Hold hands together and say a prayer of praise.

The habit of praise is formed when somebody—usually a parent—takes leadership. Pretty soon the others begin to catch on.

WHEN JOY COMES HARD

Joy and thanksgiving seem like basics. Yet I suspect not very many families manage to create a family culture that is truly joyful. Go up and down your street, listen in to the average dinner conversation, and I doubt you'll find the warm, electric current of thanks very often. A lot of families are heavy with the weight of the world.

Sometimes, paradoxically, the very same families that work hardest at living godly lives lack joy. They take life so seriously that they are a drag! In order to get joy they may need a greater dose of grace (see chapter sixteen). If you understand that life is a gift and that your failings are forgiven, you can manage the trick of being merry and serious at the same time. But if your thoughts are dominated by your performance, joy will come hard.

Sometimes the difficulty goes deeper still. Tragedy of one kind or another has robbed a family of joy, and they can't get past it. The tragedy may be external—an illness, a death, a lost job. It may be internal—a difficult marriage, tension between parents and children, personal depression. Disappointment or anger dominates family life, leaving no room for joy. "How can we sing the songs of the LORD while in a foreign land?" (Psalm 137:4).

The secret, I believe, is to start somewhere. Find some joyful or thankful practice, however small, and begin to do it. Granted, if discouragement dominates your life, every joyful practice will feel like dancing with two left feet. Nevertheless, begin to say grace at every meal, and add in a measure of thanks for those around the table. Go a little overboard in celebrating a birthday. Do something thankful, and let it stand as a hopeful beginning. Compared to the fun-loving, God-praising Joneses next door, perhaps you won't ever strike anybody as a joyful family. Compared to what you might have been, however—tired, sad, lifeless—your joy can be an astonishing achievement.

13

REST

Working Like God

"Remember the Sabbath day." EXODUS 20:8

"Jesus often withdrew to lonely places and prayed." LUKE 5:16

"Anyone who enters God's rest also rests from his own work, just as God did from his." HEBREWS 4:10

Most people I know feel harried. Perhaps life has always been so, but modern times have increased the strain. Cars and planes get us to far more places, to do more, in less time. We rush back and forth, fighting crowds. Cell phones and e-mail demand instant response. Televisions and other video tools barrage us with entertainment. Overstimulated, we go to bed too late and get up too early, trying to fit too many events into too short a day.

Walter Trobisch wrote that when we get to heaven we will be asked, "Did you have enough of everything you needed?" If we are truthful—and we will certainly be truthful in heaven—we will say, "No, Lord. We didn't have enough time."

That is our distorted perspective. In reality, God created the universe so that there exists enough time—twenty-four hours in a day is just enough—for us to do everything we must do. God has parceled out the wonderful gift of time to give us all we need.

We don't need more time; we need a way to stop and to rest. Our environment presents none. In fact, imaginative energy goes into wedging more activities into limited time—using time more efficiently so we can do more. If somebody invents a better digital calendar, you will hear about it! By contrast, no "rest crusaders" are campaigning to close the malls on Sunday or make everybody take off from work at five o'clock.

Our world will bring us no relief. Genuine rest will have to come from inside us. It will have to become a core value, shaping our lives because of its spiritual power. That is the subject of this chapter: making rest a core value through family culture. If we manage that, we will do great service to other harried families, by witnessing to another way.

NO BASEBALL ON THE SABBATH

The core value of rest harks back to the fourth commandment, "Remember the Sabbath day." We should not confuse it, however, with the traditional institution known as the Christian Sabbath.

No Christian practice was more strictly observed in eighteenth- and nineteenth-century Protestant America, and many Christians practiced a modified Sabbath well into the twentieth century. My boyhood Sundays, for example, did not allow me to listen to baseball games on the radio. Sunday afternoons I could read, play quiet games or take a nap. Most stores were closed on Sundays, but even if they had been open, my family would never have used them. On Sundays we went to church, we rested, and we did very little else.

I don't think my family was terribly unusual. I grew up hearing of Christian farmers who wouldn't work on Sundays—even when the harvest was on and rain threatened to ruin the crop. These faithful farmers were presented with awe, as heroes of the faith. Indeed, they still astonish me for their willingness to risk their livelihood for a principle.

Not everyone admired them, though. For many people, the Sabbath was a principle out of control, dedicated to oppressive religiosity. If you read old books, time and again you come across remembrances of horrid, stifling, joyless Sabbaths. I don't remember mine that way, but many people evidently did. As time went on the Sabbath strictures gradually broke down. Sunday "blue laws" were voted out. People began to play on Sundays, then to shop. Even very committed believers gradually gave up the old, inflexible rules.

Was something lost when we did away with Sabbath? Most certainly. A friend and colleague who grew up Seventh-day Adventist was asked what he missed after leaving that church. Without hesitation he said, "The Sabbath." He taught at a school where a Friday evening bell marked the beginning of Sabbath. At the sound of that bell, calm and quiet swept over the entire campus. Everything stopped. Week in, week out, the weary rested.

I think our forebears were mistaken to believe that a particular observance of a particular day is morally necessary. In many cases their religious fervor created a monster, forcing a rigidly regulated day on people who found it more hateful than restful. Still I honor their very biblical intention, to have a day dedicated to rest.

What Does God Require?

"The Sabbath," Jesus said, "was made for man, not man for the Sabbath" (Mark 2:27). With that philosophy he opposed the Pharisees, who very strictly observed the day. Yet he still regarded the Sabbath as a God-given gift. From Jesus' comments we learn that God meant the Sabbath to be observed flexibly and humanely. The rules and regulations were not to restrict but to free.

The apostle Paul made it clear that God no longer requires the day. Christians are no longer under the law, Paul wrote (Galatians 3:10-12), but they live in freedom (Galatians 5:1). The Sabbath day was only a shadow of what God intended (Colossians 2:16-17).

Rest is not a rule for us, then, something that we have to observe in a certain precise manner. Rather rest is a human need, like sleep and food—and even more, rest is an opportunity. The Scriptures say that God himself rested on the seventh day of creation (Genesis 2:2-3). That changes the whole concept of rest. God was certainly not tired or overstimulated. Why then did he rest? It must be for the same reason that he created the universe: because it was in his nature so to do. God rests, and we all can rest. Rest is built into the rhythm of existence, like the still between waves. We honor God when we imitate his restfulness.

We should not think of rest as merely an aspect of health, a response to fatigue. Just as much it is an aspect of worship, a response to God. It rests the body and the mind, and it lets us enter the presence of God, where we experience peace. He rests; we rest. If our life does not allow for this, we have strayed from the core values that God intends.

SABBATH

Didn't I just say that the Sabbath day is not required and that people have horrible memories of it? Yes, but we can certainly make a day of rest for ourselves, not because we have to but because we want to. That is exactly what some families do.

Probably the most common pattern is a variant on the old "Christian Sabbath." Families go to church, but they don't do much else. They avoid shopping. They don't work. Some families use the day to catch up with extended family or to invite people home to dinner after church. (For others, that is the exact opposite of rest. Being with family, or entertaining friends, exhausts them.) Some take long walks together. Some find working in the garden both restful and worshipful. They aren't legalistic about it in the way the Pharisees were, but they have a plan and they stick to it.

The main idea is to set a day aside—to make it different from all the others, and to design it for rest. In that day, you eliminate whatever makes you harried and frantic—committee meetings, for example, or grocery shopping. Rather, you substitute activities that renew you. For some people it's a nap. For others it's a game or a long run. For still others it's sitting down at the piano and playing worship songs. These prescriptions can flex as you and your family change. (Naps may be heaven for preschoolers and torture to teenagers.) The key is that everybody in the family knows and respects that this is our special day.

Sunday doesn't work as a day of rest for everybody. It certainly doesn't work for pastors and their families, who have to find another day of the week. For a lot of families, though, Sunday rest is liberating. Once it becomes a settled habit, it rejuvenates everybody.

My friend Philip points out that many churches have initiated Saturday evening services. With these, the day of rest can begin Saturday night and continue through an open-ended, uninterrupted Sunday, free for biking or visiting or loafing.

QUIET TIMES

"Quiet time" is a phrase often used to describe personal devotions, usually a daily period of Bible reading and prayer. It's a time-honored way of putting God first in your life. Lots of people start their day with a "quiet time" to orient everything they do around God and his will.

"Quiet times" can also function as a way of securing rest. In the "rest" orientation, you emphasize peace in the presence of God. Those who think of quiet times this way may downplay hard study and labor in prayer. Instead they emphasize meditation and stillness. Rather than actively praying through lists of missionaries during this time, they might focus on relaxing in the peace of God. It's a more Quaker-like approach.

Some families begin with a quiet moment over the breakfast table, holding hands and holding still for a few moments, capped with a prayer. Some keep the whole house quiet before breakfast—no noise, no music, little conversation—and encourage everyone to find time to rest with God as the day begins. Some encourage the same practice of quiet just before bedtime. They turn off the TV and stereo and tone down the conversations. The idea is to build rest with God into the rhythm of the day.

SPIRITUAL RETREATS

Protestant retreats have traditionally been very busy weekends, combining inspirational talks, small-group discussions and lots of conversation over meals. That can be extremely restful for some people, if only because they escape ordinary routines. Other people find the Catholic tradition of silent retreats more useful for rest and restoration. Catholic retreats (and now Protestant ones patterned after them) often involve silence at meals and quiet walks, in addition to worship services that emphasize prayer more than preaching. Most Catholic retreat centers have the Stations of the Cross laid out on the grounds to stimulate prayer and meditation. While most spiritual retreats are designed for individual restoration, it's possible to do them as a family.

NO TV

In some families, the television set is the dominant noisemaker. When it gets turned off, silence becomes very loud.

Some families (participating with the school or their community) have a "Turn Off the TV" week. You can also designate TV-free days or periods of the day. This is particularly restful if, in addition to eliminating TV distractions, families build in some rest-filled activities: family walks, music, prayer.

VACATIONS

Personally, I gravitate to two kinds of family summer vacations. One is the backpacking trip. The other is the cross-country car trip. They have this in common: you spend long hours looking at scenery, with few other distractions. In the car trip, we attend to music and books on tape, and we talk. The constant underlying reality, though, is the countryside streaming past us on the highway. It's mesmerizing, and most of the time we're quiet.

On a hike it's not so different. You can talk (if the altitude isn't so high that you lose your breath). You periodically stop together to read the map, drink water or eat a snack. The main text of the day, however, is the slowly evolving mountainscape as you climb or descend a pass. My mind wanders. Over several days of hiking I find that I think through subjects I had neglected and reflect on relationships and concerns that I had half forgotten.

Some families don't take vacations. They're too busy, they have too much to do, or they don't have any money. But if you're too busy, that is all the more reason why you need a vacation. If you don't have any money, consider camping or backpacking, which (if you borrow equipment) can be even cheaper than staying home.

Some families don't think about vacations as rest. They think of them as entertainment. Entertainment can be restful, but it often isn't. Creating a family culture of rest means figuring out what truly rests you.

I'm struck by the kind of memories family vacations leave behind in children's mind. They aren't necessarily prompted by fabulous places. A lot of the memories are of the travel to get there, of a shell found on a beach, or an ice cream cone purchased on a hot, sunny day. Some memories are of things that go wrong—car breakdowns or getting lost. Sometimes children remember the crummy, cramped motel room or the tiny motel pool more than they remember the destination resort. What makes a family vacation valuable isn't summed up in the travel brochure. It has more to do with family togetherness, with change from ordinary routines, with adventure. For children as well as parents, these things are restorative.

FAMILY ACTIVITIES AROUND HOME

Rest isn't just for vacations. Some families schedule regular activities that they find restful. They'll break up a busy week with some time reading aloud together, walking, biking, picnicking, driving in the country, going for a swim, making music together or watching the stars.

I find the beach to be tremendously restful. In our part of California, beaches are too cold and foggy for sunbathing. Walking or exploring tide pools is more like it. The pounding of the waves and the bracing wind seem to wash my mind clean. Yet life is so busy that I don't get to the beach often. I need to remember to set aside time, with family or alone, because I need the rest.

CHURCH

Attending church on a weekly basis can be the most restoring habit a family has, but many families have to work at making it so. Begin with getting there. If different members of your family have very different senses of timing, getting to church can be an exercise in anger and frustration. That isn't restful. Speaking for myself, I had to learn that when I had done everything I could to get the family ready, I had best sit down and quietly read while others finished getting ready. It didn't help them or me if I fussed. I am better off arriving late in a peaceful frame of mind than making the opening hymn with my brain sizzling.

Resting while worshiping also takes attention. If you let yourself be distracted or annoyed, if you practice writing critical reviews of the music in your head, you will gain little rest. I have yet to attend a worship service that offered nothing—no song, prayer or sermon nugget—that could benefit me. If you go looking to pour your soul into the worship of the living God, you will find rest in worship. Attitudes are under our control. The service is not.

Finally, when you come home from church, you need to let rest carry through. It helps to take some time on arriving home, letting yourself relax before rushing into lunch. That gives worship's benefits time to sink deep within. My family usually comments on the worship service, which is a natural activity, but one that can easily turn negative. With a disciplined effort, though, we can focus on what we appreciated.

SAYING NO

Nobody can rest without saying no. Modern life offers so much stimulation, so many possibilities, that one could sign up for educational and useful activities thirty-six hours a day. It requires discipline to say no and leave time to rest.

Many families need structured help to do it. You can systematically rely on other people—family members or one or two close friends—to help you screen opportunities. As a matter of policy, you just don't take on new activities until you've talked it over with your advisor group. This gives you an answer for the pleading voice on the phone.

I also rely on a twenty-four-hour waiting period. If somebody asks me to do something, I usually ask for twenty-four hours to think and pray about it. Many times, by doing that I have avoided taking on too much. I find it too easy to say yes on the spot.

FINDING REST

You really do have enough time. God would never ask you to do the impossible, so you must be able to do what you need to do—and do it correctly and peaceably—in the time you have been given.

That is easy advice to offer—and hard advice to take. Additionally, while raising children should slow you down, most people feel speeded up. The world plays on our ambitions for our children. We don't want them to miss out, and so we try to do too much. We only manage to pass on our anxieties to our children, who never learn how to stop and rest either.

Make no mistake: you have to *learn* to rest. You have to learn the mental and spiritual discipline of putting aside all the urgencies of life simply to relax, regroup, enjoy life and enjoy God. It helps to know that God does it, that his efforts to create the world included a day of making nothing. He is a working God, and he is a resting God. When your family culture incorporates the core value of rest, you draw closer to God's Spirit. So do your children.

14

CARE FOR GOD'S CREATION

The First Commandment in the Bible

"Rule over the fish of the sea and the birds of the air and over every living creature." GENESIS 1:28

"God saw all that he had made, and it was very good." GENESIS 1:31

"May the glory of the LORD endure forever; may the LORD rejoice in his works." PSALM 104:31

"Look at the birds of the air; they do not sow or reap or store away in barns, and yet your heavenly Father feeds them. Are you not much more valuable than they?" MATTHEW 6:26

"You shall not murder." EXODUS 20:13

In recent years we have seen a remarkable growth in concern for nature. Endangered species have caught the public attention, and huge amounts of money are spent on environmental impact studies. In schools, whales and butterflies are greatly honored. Those who wear fur must do so defensively. On television, animal sex and violence rate nearly as much coverage as the human varieties. *National Geographic* specials bring exotic species and environments into our living rooms.

Children grow up with a great emphasis on ecology. They learn much
that is good, backed by a cluster of vague and conflicting ideals. For example, regarding themselves: are human beings the great brutes of creation, despoiling everything they touch? Or are humans the protectors
and defenders of other creatures—the great ecologists?

Some environmental activists blame Christianity for spoiling our environment, chiefly by contributing the idea that humans have been put in
charge of the other creatures. That is said to be arrogant and unscientific.
In reality we are just one creature out of millions, they say, and nothing
special. Yet if that is so, why should we be ecologically sensitive? If we are
not in charge of the creatures, why are we supposed to preserve them?

Somewhere deep down, everyone knows that human beings are not
like other creatures. We have unique gifts and responsibilities. When we
teach care for God's creation as a core value, we help children know
where they stand.

GOD'S FIRST COMMAND

"Be fruitful and increase in number; fill the earth and subdue it." That
was God's first command to the first human beings, according to Genesis
1:28. It was followed immediately by a second, related command: "Rule
over the fish of the sea and the birds of the air and over every living creature that moves on the ground."

Have you ever noticed how absurd these words sound, given the situation? The prospect that two lone people could ever fill the vast planet
must have seemed ridiculous to them, standing before tens of thousands
of miles of untouched wilderness. For thousands of years thereafter, until comparatively recent times, the globe included vast stretches that
were practically uninhabited—certainly not filled.

And then, how would humans rule over the fish of the sea and the
birds of the air? Fish do not come when you whistle, and you cannot
herd birds. The fish and the birds are among the least controllable of
all God's creatures; they live in water where humans cannot long sur-
vive and in air where humans cannot go. Just how could humans rule
over these?

It is a wonder to me that these very ancient words, recorded in some of the very oldest known documents, have become so obviously relevant. Their meaning was obscure for millennia but today seems easily understandable.

Only in the last century could it truly be said that humanity has filled the earth, dominating the globe to such an extent that we now manage fish and bird populations. What was unthinkable for Eve and Adam has become commonplace for the National Bureau of Fisheries. Truly, we do rule over the fish of the sea and the birds of the air.

Genesis makes one point very clear: we are *supposed* to rule over the creatures of the earth, *supposed* to fill the earth. Humanity is not an unfortunate accident for the fate of the planet, but God's intention.

In biblical thinking, the command to rule the earth does not give us carte blanche to destroy wild creatures. On the contrary, it defines our responsibility. In the Bible a ruler is not a law unto himself. A ruler is appointed by God to provide for the welfare of his subjects. If humans are appointed to rule, as the Bible says, we must see to it that the world is cared for as God wants it cared for. God cares for even the common sparrow (Matthew 10:29). Surely we should as well.

PETS

Our pets are different from wild creatures, for they have become interconnected with us and dependent on us. From the Bible's perspective, however, this is a virtue. Isaiah proclaims a vision of God's redemption wherein all God's creatures live in harmony, the lamb with the lion (Isaiah 11:6-9). The closest I ever see to this is my golden retriever and striped tabby cat lying together at my feet in my living room.

Through pets children learn to take care of animals. They also learn to love animals. It helps when children take responsibility for training, feeding, walking and cleaning up after their pets. Parents can easily do this themselves, but the children who carry through become more involved with the animals and more understanding of their nature. My youngest son learned a great deal about the complex chemistry of the environment through keeping an aquarium and later an outdoor pond.

Quite a few fish died in the process, but he gained new eyes for the complexity of a fish's habitat.

FARM ANIMALS

Animals raised by rural children for 4-H projects are not exactly pets, since they are generally sold and butchered in the end. Just as with pets, though, such animals give the children who raise and care for them a very practical sense of animals' needs. Even the slaughter has its benefits: children grasp very personally that meat does not come wrapped in cellophane. Raising animals for food can help families gain respect for the life of animals. It does not usually make vegetarians out of children, but does increase their understanding and appreciation of food.

These projects take a lot of time and attention, they are messy, and disease or injury can very easily become part of the learning experience. They offer powerful lessons in our interaction with the animal kingdom. Not just eagles, wolves and whales are God's creatures; so are cows and sheep.

GARDENING

With a vegetable garden, children see the whole life cycle in a few months: germination, growing, fruiting and dying. The depredations of insects and disease are dramatic. The fact that you get to eat whatever the garden produces increases interest.

Some children get a row of their own in the family garden, to plant and care for as they like. Others share in the family garden by planting, watering and weeding.

Any kind of garden can stimulate interest and understanding, if you work at it. Calvin DeWitt, professor of ecology at the University of Wisconsin, takes pride in the fact that his lawn contains dozens of species of grass (rather than the three or four you get in a bag of seed). What looks like an ordinary, scruffy expanse of turf turns out, under close inspection, to be an ecosystem of its own.

Even garden problems can pique your appreciation for creation. I have spent the last few years worrying over my geraniums and a species of caterpillar that drills holes in the bud for each individual bloom. I wish to do away with these bugs, but they have won my respect and have thus far defeated me. Meanwhile I have found their life patterns very interesting.

OUTDOOR RECREATION

Pets and gardens are part of life at home. Some families are better suited to outdoor recreation. I've recommended this kind of activity several times in this book, as it fits a number of goals. And here's another: if parents and kids get out into nature, they're likely to enjoy God's creation and also come to understand it better.

Growing up, I loved backpacking for the scenery, the adventure and the athletic challenge. But in the process I became curious about other things. I learned some fundamental geology, plus the names of most of the wildflowers I saw in the mountains. In other words, outdoor recreation opened the door for understanding more about creation.

Any outdoor sport has the same potential, whether it be hiking, biking, canoeing, snorkeling or something else. Of course, some people spend a great portion of their lives outdoors and seem to see nothing. A family that has a culture of outdoor sports, though, has great opportunities to learn respect for nature, especially if a parent-in-charge is learning and sharing what he or she learns.

BIRDS, FLOWERS, ROCKS

There's no better way to gain understanding and love for God's creation than by walking with a book in hand, learning as you go. The book of Genesis says that Adam's first assignment was to name the animals. The point of this exercise is not explained in the Bible, but I think it was intended to help Adam in his job of ruling the creation. When you name something, you pay attention to its individual characteristics.

I know this: pretty flowers never had much meaning to me until I got a wildflower book and began to learn their names. Then they became like friends to me. When you see an old friend and call her by name, love floods in. Some families learn names of flowers, trees, birds and rocks together.

Whale Watching

While I've clumped together other kinds of nature activity, I think whale watching deserves a category of its own. When you see a whale in nature, you cannot help being amazed, almost overwhelmed. They have the impact of an earthquake, a tornado or a volcano—but unlike those, you can schedule whale watching. Whales remind us how small we are. Their wildness reminds us how much of creation remains outside our understanding and control and in God's hands alone.

Armchair Travelers

You can also learn respect for God's creation while sitting at home. Consider watching *National Geographic* TV specials as a family. If parents take an interest, children usually will too. The shows open wider vistas for everyone, showing the exotic and hidden parts of nature.

A subscription to *National Geographic* magazine serves the same purpose. Families can look at the pictures together. Various coffee-table books on the beauties of nature attract children and serve to awaken them to the world of God's making. These publications are expensive, but some families make the investment just to nudge their family toward a deeper appreciation for creation.

Science Museums

Almost every major city has some kind of science museum, as do many university towns. Aquariums and zoos are highly varied and interesting. You can visit hands-on science museums and museums of natural history. Some families put these places on their list everywhere they go.

Family Councils

The care of creation is no simple matter. It includes many controversial issues, some of which affect family decisions. Here's a list of issues that can easily become controversial for families:

- simple living
- vegetarianism
- organic foods

- recycling
- use of pesticides and fertilizers in the garden
- car purchases
- genetically modified foods

Some families try to bring the whole family into these issues by holding a family council on them. It doesn't have to be a decision-making body; it can also be an advisory council to the executive committee (read: the parents). If you want to go that route, though, you had better pay close attention to what your advisors say. Otherwise they'll revolt.

You can get children to do additional research on any of these subjects. Through that experience they can engage with real information and begin to understand the sheer complexity of the world God has made. Some families will find it very interesting and pleasurable to work these issues together.

WHY A CORE VALUE?

I have the impression that many families take the matter of care for God's creation very lightly. They see it as a "nice" value but not crucial. Similarly, many think of ecology as a "nice" movement which they are in favor of, but to which they are not terribly dedicated.

Yet care for creation is the first command of the Bible, and it offers the largest and most challenging responsibility imaginable. Think of Adam and Eve, two children of God on a vast, wild planet. The task is overwhelming.

It remains so. The complexity of our biosphere and the dynamism of human activity make care for creation a bracing challenge. It meets us in whatever we do, wherever we live. This core value spurs us to use our God-given gifts—our brains, our creativity—to his glory. If you want your children to reach their greatest potential, you will want them to put this challenge at their core.

15

CONTENTMENT
Finding Peace with What You Have

"You shall not covet." EXODUS 20:17

*"Do not worry about your life, what you will eat or drink; . . .
do not worry about tomorrow."* MATTHEW 6:25, 34

*"Be content with what you have, because God has said,
'Never will I leave you.' "* HEBREWS 13:5

"Let the peace of Christ rule in your hearts." COLOSSIANS 3:15

Most of my childhood Christmas memories are happy. One moment, though, repeated year after year, always left me sad. It came on Christmas morning, just after we had opened all the gifts. Surrounded by the litter of wrapping paper and by piles of presents, groggy from waking up at daybreak, I suddenly felt the weight of a hopeless fact: Christmas was over.

As a child I longed for Christmas. Every day I examined the packages under the tree, wondering what happiness they represented. Now I knew. I had torn off the colored paper and—here was the terrible truth—I was not satisfied.

I wanted more. Or at least I wanted something, a nameless gift to fill my longings. Despite all that I had received, I did not feel filled up.

This feeling of discontent is not just for children at Christmas. It is well summarized in the words of a very wealthy man who, when asked just how much money it would take to satisfy him, said, "A little more."

How many of us could echo him. If it's not money we want, it's a little more success. A little more physical beauty. A little more love.

Some people spend their entire life plagued by a state of discontent. Their spouse disappoints them. They don't like their job. They wish for different looks. Their children let them down. Their friends aren't in the circle they would like. I've known people, and you probably have too, who become so sour that nobody wants to be around them. They are "glass-half-empty" people.

It has little to do with what they have or what they achieve. It has to do with a deeper, spiritual condition. If we could pass on the secret of contentment to our children, what gift could be more valuable?

YOU CAN'T ALWAYS GET WHAT YOU WANT

I once had a chance to interview several major league baseball players. I am a baseball fan, and I was excited to rub up against these idols. They have it all: they're young, athletic, rich and famous. They live a boyhood dream, augmented by some very grown-up extras. People adore them. Women offer themselves to them. Their suitcases are delivered straight from the airplane to their hotel rooms.

Are ballplayers contented? Well, some are. Most are not. I was struck by how often they seemed insecure and frustrated. Their marriages have the same troubles as everybody else's. They get mad at their bosses. They worry. They wander around the house in a mood.

Experience shows that the richest and most successful people are not necessarily truly satisfied. Don't look for the secret of contentment on *Lifestyles of the Rich and Famous.*

There's another image of contentment that has grown quite popular: the Buddha. Buddhism approaches contentment from a completely different angle. I am by no means an expert, but my understanding is that a Buddhist recognizes that outward success cannot satisfy. Instead Buddhists turns their attention inward. Buddhists are supposed to do away with troubles by extinguishing desire. If they want nothing, how can they be dissatisfied? That is why the classic statue of the Buddha shows him quiet and self-contained. The Buddha sits with his eyes closed. He wants nothing, so he is content.

The Christian agrees with Buddhists that the secret of contentment is spiritual, but the Christian idea is not to extinguish desire. We retain desires, not only for ourselves but for the world. Our idea is to have faith, cooperating with God. Our God will not leave the world to its meaningless rotation, we believe. He will redeem it. We can be content in this troubled world only because we are content with him and we trust him.

The apostle Paul put it eloquently: "I have learned the secret of being content in any and every situation, whether well fed or hungry, whether living in plenty or in want. I can do everything through him who gives me strength" (Philippians 4:12-13). Paul means that his contentment is not affected by circumstances because he depends on an unchangeable reality: the power of Jesus Christ. Focused on Jesus, he knows that he will get what he needs. Trusting in Christ, he need not worry.

Paul had not extinguished desire. He was a very ambitious and hardworking person, with tremendous hopes and dreams. He gave every bit of his energy to them. His letters to churches, which we read in the Bible, brim with energetic plans and advice. Sometimes he felt terribly distressed by what he observed. However, Paul understood that God's ideas were bigger than his and that God's power was greater than his. Whatever the circumstances, good or bad, he could look hopefully into the future and ask God, "What's next?"

An Example of Contentment

My friend Harold Myra is an example for me. As president of a multi-million-dollar magazine publishing company, he has achieved a great deal. However, "driven" he is not. I'm confident that if it all went under tomorrow, Harold would barely raise an eyebrow. He's glad for what he's done, and proud of it too, but his life doesn't depend on it.

I've seen Harold go through many difficulties, both at work and in his family. Of course these affect him, but he doesn't protest, "Why me?" nor does he act as though it's all his fault and his responsibility. He simply looks to do what he can. He's very charitable, even to those who are making his life miserable. In the face of overwhelming difficulties, he seems to believe that somehow, through God's grace, his own limited abilities will be enough. Or, if not, Harold isn't afraid to suffer. He doesn't panic, and he doesn't turn the attention to himself. He just keeps on.

Harold seems to know at the core of his being that the world isn't about Harold Myra. Rather, he has faith to know that the world is about God's grace. Consequently Harold is content, whether he's at the top or seems to be headed for the bottom. He's not content with leaving things as they are—if he were, he would never have the motivation to accomplish anything. He's content with God's control of the universe.

Harold is a quiet man who works behind the scenes, often in unspectacular ways. Truthfully, contentment never is very spectacular. It's a value that lies quietly underneath—a foundation for wonderful deeds. That is all the more reason why we should pay attention to contentment. The world around us never will.

I SEE, I WANT

In thinking about contentment, a good place to start is the grocery store. Put a three-year-old child in the seat of a grocery cart, and what happens as you wheel her through the store? The child grabs at stuff and asks for candy, gum, toys. It's an automatic response: I see, I want. Parents can train children not to grab or whine, but they are working against the flow.

That's partly because human beings are consumers by nature, but also because the grocery store planners do a magnificent job of stimulating the response. They put attractive toys, candy, gum and sugar-saturated cereals right at the child's eye level. They especially make the checkout line a gauntlet. They are selling candy, not helping parents raise contented children.

So the problem of contentment has two sides. One is spiritual: how do I wean children (or myself) from "see it, want it"? The other is tactical: how do I live in a world that tries, for commercial reasons, to stimulate dissatisfaction?

The patterns get learned very early: in the grocery store shopping cart, at home when toys must be shared with cousins, under the Christmas tree when pouts come after the presents are opened. Family culture can lay down tracks of contentment that make it natural to trust in God's goodness. Family culture can help nurture an instinctive reaction of faith rather than worry or covetousness.

LIMIT OPPORTUNITIES FOR COVETOUSNESS

The last of the Ten Commandments declares, "You shall not covet." Coveting is the opposite of contentment. It has to do with desiring what isn't properly yours: "your neighbor's wife, or his manservant or maidservant, his ox or donkey, or anything that belongs to your neighbor" (Exodus 20:17).

In the New Testament, *lust* is a word very similar to *coveting*. The Greek word for "lust" doesn't necessarily have any sexual connotation. It doesn't even necessarily have an immoral meaning. It simply means, "strong desire." When does desire become immoral? When you're longing for something that God doesn't intend for you. When your longing drives you to do what you shouldn't. We call that lust.

Covetousness and lust are diseases of the mind. They infect our thoughts with their virus, which damages our rationality. Pornography offers a good example of how the disease works. Does the appeal of pornography make any sense? Is it reasonable to believe that you could satisfy your sexual needs by watching somebody else perform sex on film? The opposite is true. Pornography is not designed in any way to satisfy. The purpose of pornography is to incite more dissatisfaction, to make you want more pornography. It is a virus that feeds on legitimate desires, twisting them and turning them against us.

Another example: Is it rational to believe that you will be happy if you acquire the car/clothes/stereo you desire? We all know it is not. Yet advertising works to incite the irrational and compulsive thought that we would be happy if we could gain certain possessions.

Some people lust for closeness with their extended family. Some people lust for fame as a preacher of the gospel. You can lust after almost anything. If you want something so much that it makes you act irrationally, that is lust.

Martin Luther said that he couldn't keep the birds from flying over his head, but he could keep them from making nests in his hair. One role of family culture is to shoo the birds out of our hair. Irrational desires are bound to enter our brains, but we don't have to entertain them.

LIMIT SHOPPING

This is easy for me to write, because I don't particularly like shopping. A lot of people do, however. For many people, going to the mall is the modern equivalent of market day. It's a social act, a way to see and be seen.

The problem is that shopping puts you into the orbit of people dedicated to stimulating lust. Masters of merchandising study how to present stuff so that you want it even when you don't necessarily need it. The more you shop, the more these images get planted in your brain. Even if you resist temptation once, your mind will return to the same images. Back to the mall you'll go! For some people merchandise acts almost like pornography, with its enticing, addictive quality.

Maybe shopping isn't that for you. Maybe it is purely relaxation. But does it affect the rest of your family in the same relaxing way? Remember, our focus is *family* culture.

I said I don't like shopping, but I do enjoy grocery shopping. That's where I had my earliest experiences shopping with children, and where I learned how artfully grocery stores offer impulse items within kids' reach. Early on, I decided not to buy any of that stuff, ever. Why would we? None of it was good for my kids, and none of it made them really happy. Away from the grocery store, they wouldn't even think to want gum. For a five-year-old mind, it was purely a matter of material lust: See-it-want-it. When we stopped buying, the lust practically disappeared. The kids still liked to go shopping, but they tended not to make the experience miserable by whining for candy.

Truthfully, I was a sucker buying stuff for my kids—particularly baseball gloves and soccer balls, even ice cream and candy. In the grocery store, though, I became an absolutist, trying to break the link between see-it and buy-it.

In the olden days, people went shopping once a week, on Saturdays.

That's because, if they worked regular hours, the stores were open to them only on Saturdays. Now, of course, stores are open for our continuous convenience. Some families establish a single shopping day, once a week. That makes them plan ahead and do less impulsive buying. Most of all, it keeps them out of the stores, and keeps those images of acquisition out of their brains.

Another way is to shop from a list. Some families make it a rule not to buy anything unless they have written it down ahead of time. That means they really want or need it—the idea wasn't stimulated by the act of shopping.

Some families just don't go to warehouse stores. These warehouse clubs offer great prices, but they have perfected the art of getting you to buy more than you need. By packaging huge quantities at bargain prices, they get many a family to roll out of the parking lot with a trunk full of stuff they don't even have room to store.

More than a few families have put away the credit and debit cards. They only pay cash, which tends to slow down their shopping splurges. For some, credit is intrinsically linked to their love of shopping. If they have to pay cash, they don't even want to shop.

If you're going to cut down on shopping you may need to add some other activity to replace its social function. Some families go to a lot of high school sporting events. Some go biking or hiking together. Some do farmers markets or garage sales. (Yes, they spend money, but the experience is a lot less likely to stimulate lust for things.)

LIMIT GIFTS

This will sound strange to many people: One of the greatest stimuli to material lust is mutual gift giving. Don't believe me? Go through your bulging closet. I think you will find that a great proportion of your overabundance was bought, not with your money, but with somebody else's. Meanwhile a great deal of what's in the closets of your family and friends came from *your* wallet. This is why retail businesses absolutely depend on Christmas shopping, sometimes for half their revenue. If we took away Christmas, birthdays and anniversaries, would there be any economy left?

Generosity is one of our most beautiful impulses, and in America we have made it a competitive sport. We don't feel right buying impulsively for ourselves (or we can't think of anything we need), so we have all reached an unstated agreement: we will buy impulsively for each other.

Evil often works this way. It takes our most noble instinct and twists it so that we end up causing harm. I feel ever so loving when I give extravagantly to my wife, my siblings, my children, my parents, my friends. And so do they when they give generously to me. We are thinking of others! Yet somehow the end result is that we all have nicer clothes and more things than we would buy for ourselves. We spend far more of our income on gifts for people who don't need them than we do on gifts for truly needy and hungry people. In the end we don't own the stuff—the stuff owns us. It owns our attention, it owns our time, and it soaks up the cash with which we might be generous to needy people.

There are several ways in which family culture can cut out competitive gift giving while keeping the spirit of generosity. One is to draw names for major holidays, so that each person gives only one gift, on a rotating basis, to one family member. Some families pull names out of a hat within their nuclear family. Other families do it for all the cousins, uncles and aunts.

Another way is to donate to favorite charities. Instead of giving superfluous gifts to each other, you make a gift to the charity in the name of your family member. Some organizations allow you to purchase, for example, a flock of twenty hens for an impoverished family in Bolivia, to provide eggs for the family to eat and sell. The organization provides an attractive card for your family member explaining the gift given in his or her name. Charitable giving could become competitive too, but it's not clear that this ever happens. Even if it did, would that be such a bad thing?

A third way is to cap the price of gifts at, say, ten dollars. Or, you can insist on "priceless" gifts, presented through an attractive card or handmade coupon. A priceless gift might be a certificate for a walk together in the park or a game of catch. It might be good for an afternoon looking at old photographs. It might be a clean garage or a washed and waxed car. It might be a picture reframed. Generally, priceless gifts involve time—which we may find the costliest gift of all. Interestingly enough, priceless gifts don't seem susceptible to competitive giving. Instead they have a calming effect.

Limit TV

Between the shows and the commercials—which take nearly a third of air time—television is perfectly designed to make you dissatisfied. Your spouse, your car, your furniture, your waistline, your bald spot—none of it looks good after an evening watching TV. I'm not saying TV offers nothing good. I'm saying that TV makes you think there is nothing good in your life. Channel surfing is the ultimate expression of this discontent. I've been there! It's a strange experience, flipping aimlessly from one channel to the next, searching for something to entertain or distract you. Channel surfing always leaves you with an empty spot in your spirit.

One of my friends remembers his toddler staring blankly at the screen. She could barely talk, but she put her few words to good use. Every time she saw an advertisement, she pointed toward it and said, "I want one!" When she graduated to saying, "I want two!" he knew something had to be done.

In our family, we jerked the cable. That meant no TV at all. (We live in hills where, without cable, you can't get a signal.) We did it because one of my children was particularly vulnerable to channel surfing. He actually was wise enough to request the change. I probably felt the loss most, because I love to watch sports.

Life without TV was hard for a while, but now, years into the experiment, none of us wants to go back. Yes, I still miss watching baseball, but it's absolutely amazing how much more time you have without a TV. And, more important for our present purposes, life without TV feels less artificial. You gain a greater sense of choosing for yourself what you want to do, rather than being dragged along by video hypnosis. (Bear in mind that if you really want to see a program, you can generally get one of your friends or neighbors to let you in to view it. You don't *have* to miss anything.)

Less drastic approaches can be used. Some families record shows on the VCR. That way they watch only what really interests them—no channel surfing—and they can fast-forward through the commercials.

Lots of families limit the hours of TV, either by setting a number of hours allowed per week or by letting each family member choose one show per week for the whole family. (That tends to make TV a more family-oriented event, rather than a narcotic indulged in privately.)

One friend of mine invented a gizmo whereby a stationary bike got hooked to a power switch, so you could see TV only if somebody rode the bike. He said the Super Bowl gave him the workout of his life!

Increase Opportunities for Generosity

To this point I have concentrated on the negative side of teaching contentment—that is, limiting lust. We need a positive side too. Some activities help us develop trust in God. They take our eyes off ourselves and point our vision toward God and what he cares about.

Many of the practices described in chapter four, "Concern for Others," help stimulate contentment. When you serve others, you think of yourself less. And when you get to know people who have very little, you see the triviality of the things you're tempted to lust after.

One reason people shy away from the poor is that they fear feeling guilty. They know how they hate seeing a homeless person slouched at a traffic light, begging. They don't want to expose themselves to more of that.

In reality, though, they might feel *less* guilt if they got closer to the poor. When I first moved to Kenya I remember looking forward to a first-hand encounter with dire poverty. I had lived a thoroughly middle-class existence, and I felt guilty about it. I thought a close exposure to truly poor people would shame me into living more simply. I expected to have my sense of guilt increased. That, I thought, would be unpleasantly good for me.

My experience didn't turn out quite the way I expected. I encountered plenty of dire poverty, far more dramatic poverty than any I could find at home. My exposure was often deeply personal too: I got to know poor people and their families, and sometimes I was able to help them. At the same time I frequently experienced frustration at my impotence in making a real difference.

In the end, though, the experience didn't make me more con-science-stricken about my life as a wealthy American. I came to see that poverty and wealth, while important, are not so important as I had thought. Not to underrate money, but the most important factors in a person's well-being are spiritual. Some poor people I met were, in fact, very happy—happier than most rich people. (I already knew that many rich people were desperately unhappy.) Even at the boundaries of extreme poverty, income has limited significance. It matters, but other factors matter far more.

Anyone closely involved with the needy will have a similar shift in thinking. It doesn't make you any less concerned for economic justice. It doesn't diminish your desire to help the poor. It does, however, make you aware that life is much more than food and clothing. It does make you more aware that we live by the word of God, not by bread alone.

That's why getting your family involved with the poor, through soup kitchens or homeless shelters, through nursing homes or foster care, can encourage a sense of contentment. If you see the poor from a distance, superficially, you may misread the situation and think that money is terribly important. Get to know people, and you'll understand that money doesn't begin to define their lives. Nor does it define yours.

LIVING SIMPLY

Generation after generation of young Americans discovers "simple living." They begin wearing second-hand clothes, eating beans and rice, and keeping the thermostat south of 62 degrees. They recycle, use public transit and engage in long and earnest discussions of world poverty.

This tends to be a short-term commitment. Most people abandon simple living later in life, often about the time they get married and have children. I could make several guesses about why most people don't stick to simple living, but one observation I am sure of: contentment doesn't necessarily come with simple living. If it did, nobody would give it up!

Contentment is a state of mind, not a standard of living. Nevertheless, simple living can have its value in training the mind toward contentment. This is true under only two conditions: that the emphasis is on "simple," not "cheap," and that giving money away is held in higher esteem than saving money.

To the extent that I learned to live more simply during my years in Kenya, it was through finding that living simply is often quite pleasurable. We didn't have many things because we didn't have much income, and also because many aspects of material culture just weren't available. Life is less hectic when you live simply.

Most missionaries I have met around the world live simply. Hardly any missionaries I have met around the world are focused on living simply. They are focused on the calling God has given them; they live simply because it makes sense in their environment. Nowhere in the Bible are we told to choose a simple lifestyle. Rather the Bible warns us not to be consumed by things, to practice generosity, and to be content with whatever we have. A choice of simple lifestyle can help us toward those ends.

John Wesley urged Christians to "earn all you can, save all you can, give all you can." According to him, if somebody pays you ten million dollars in stock options you should be glad. That means you can give away $9,950,000 or so. The virtue lies in giving to others.

Most of us don't dream of stock options, but by living simply we can gain the means to be generous. Generous people experience contentment. As my mother (who never had much money) likes to say, "I always feel wealthy when I'm writing checks to charity. I have so much money I can give it away!"

Families develop many habits to save money and live simply. One is meals on a budget. Though food is probably a small part of your expenses, it is a very noticeable part. The whole family experiences the difference when you spend less on food, and this makes them aware of simple living. Some families make the children responsible for a week (or a weekend) of meals. On a regular rotation the children get a set budget to work from. Challenge them to save money so the remainder can be donated to a local hunger program! (Make sure you review the menus to see that everybody gets enough nutritious food.)

You can think up many variations on this. Establish a "soda fund" that kicks in a quarter every time you drink a glass of water instead of a Coke. (You'll cut dental bills too.) The money can add up to impressive contributions.

Or make one dinner a week a World Meal. That means you eat beans and rice, and the money saved goes into a family anti-hunger fund. You can probably support a child through World Vision or Compassion with this fund alone.

The point isn't so much the amount of money you give, though that can add up. The point is the habit of life, which aims not to consume but to give. It makes a lasting memory.

Some families make a family habit of saving money on cars. Again, this is a very public form of simple living, which the whole family feels directly. And it's a learning experience. Your kids may have a hard time believing it, but they can experience a certain cachet in owning the oldest car in the parking lot. As a matter of fact, almost any car gets to be a classic if you hang onto it long enough.

We have a sixteen-year-old, four-cylinder, standard-transmission minivan that all three kids learned to drive on. It's got dents in back and a cracked window. Early on it embarrassed my kids to no end, but eventually they got to be proud of it. It achieved nearly legendary status at the high school. With all its creaks and groans it seems nearly sentient. I'm not suggesting that old cars are for everybody, but that they are an element of family culture that works for some. It did for us. It was "what the Staffords do," and it taught our kids a valuable lesson in the pleasures of making do.

Note the word *pleasure*. There's contentment in finding happiness with an old car. The mental practice extends to other areas of life.

SPIRITUAL DISCIPLINES

Contentment is a spiritual condition, strengthened through spiritual disciplines. All of the classic spiritual disciplines help our spiritual weakness, encouraging faith. Some lend themselves particularly to the family culture of contentment.

Family fasting. Some families practice fasting during the season of Lent, giving up (fasting from) some particular pleasure for the days leading up to Easter. Some do it individually but tell each other what they've sacrificed, whether chocolate or coffee or desserts or sodas. Other families agree to fast together—perhaps giving up desserts or eating rice and beans for dinner.

You can also agree as a family to take a day of complete fasting—twenty-four hours with only fruit juices, for example. Fasting has a negative side, giving something up, and a positive side, making more time to pray.

Fasting reminds everyone that life is more than food. It turns your attention toward God. It stimulates meditation, prayer and personal inventory. Together these can help train the mind and the spirit toward contentment.

Counting your blessings. Another family practice is to keep track together of the blessings you see in your life. The effect over time can be profound. We have so much—of course we should be content! Counting your blessings forces you to take inventory.

Some families take time in their family prayers for a periodic inventory of blessings. They may do it every Monday, for example, simply sharing and praying together about whatever they feel grateful for. Other families share at Thanksgiving or on birthdays. Car trips and vacations offer particular opportunities to review the past year and note down all you have to be grateful for. The first few times you try this, it may not go easily. After all, brushing your teeth doesn't come easily at first either. If you keep it up, though, counting your blessings will become expected. You will even look forward to it!

Daily prayer. Finally, I want to mention praying together regularly. No habit has more potential for teaching contentment.

I learned this during my years in Kenya. I had agreed to go and start a Christian magazine for young people. I raised money from many of my family and friends in order to cover our expenses and start-up costs, with the understanding that the magazine would need to become self-sufficient.

It was a great adventure for me. I had never started anything before, never been the "boss." It was exciting to work in an entirely new environment, learning as I went. Along with my colleague Bob Butt, I did a careful study of the market conditions. We hired a staff team. We began to publish, and one marvelous day *Step Magazine* appeared on the street corners of cities throughout Kenya.

The magazine was slow to catch on, though. As expenses mounted and income lagged, the realization sank in that we might fail. We had set a machine in motion, and now we had very limited control over the results. Doing our very best might still be inadequate. We had to work hard, publishing the best magazine we could, while simply waiting to see whether people would buy it and advertisers would use it. I felt quite helpless.

I had never before felt so responsible for something. I was responsible to those I had employed. I was responsible to those who had contributed money. I felt deep agony at the idea of coming home a failure. I'd like to say that my concern was to communicate with thousands of Kenyans through a Christian magazine; but I think that the truth was less wonderful. I didn't want to be humiliated.

The burden grew heavier. I got so anxious I could barely get through the day. Depression hung over me. I was so worried I could hardly think straight. That was when I learned in a new way to pray—to depend on prayer like breathing. Dogged, daily prayer was the only way to get through each day. Minute by minute God sustained me through prayer.

Families have lots of different praying traditions, fitting their personal style. The main question is, do you have one? Nothing else can so help your family gain the habit of contentment.

THE QUESTION OF AMBITION

I have somewhat mixed feelings about teaching contentment to my children. I'm very ambitious for them. Because I love them, I want them to do well in every department. I want them to get the best grades, to win all their games and to make many good friends. When they don't succeed I'm full of advice for how they could try harder, work smarter, plan and strategize to improve their fortunes. Frankly, I do my share of stimulating dissatisfaction. I'm not fueling a candy-and-gum fixation, but I'm tempted by a success-and-achievement fixation.

I don't want my children to be content with mediocrity. When they don't seem troubled by failure, it troubles me. There's a fine line between contentment and laziness.

Is there a proper, godly way to be ambitious? I find it helpful to reflect deeply on what the apostle Paul meant by contentment. He certainly wasn't encouraging a don't-care attitude. He was ambitious himself. He threw himself body and soul into the cause of Christ.

That is the first lesson we can glean from Paul: make sure you're ambitious for the right aims. If my child is a musician or a carpenter or an engineer, he or she should aim to do the very best possible work—not in order to stand above others but in order to contribute to others. A musician should be ambitious to make beautiful and moving music. A carpenter should be ambitious to do skillful work. Yet many kinds of ambition are selfish, vain and purely material. They are just an extension of what a child feels in the grocery cart.

Paul's second lesson has to do with faith. There's a vast difference between energy expended out of anxiety, fear and rivalry and energy expended out of trust. Paul encouraged trust in God. Rather than sapping energy, trust can add to your energy. It helps you relax rather than worry. If you trust, failure doesn't disable you; you know the results don't depend just on you. I want my children to grow up ambitious because they trust God to do wonderful things.

If I were to draw a portrait of contentment, it wouldn't show somebody lying in a hammock, sipping lemonade. I would show a baseball player at bat, confident in his abilities, sure that he is meant to be in this joyful spot. He won't get a hit every time, but he knows that he will get his share. He wants to succeed, but not in order to show himself as better than the rest of his team. He wants to contribute to his team. Therefore he is happy and relaxed as he focuses on the ball and swings with all his skill and strength.

Not many of us experience such contentment. We get anxious, we feel envious, we act competitive. We experience disappointment on Christmas morning and on many other days. Our children learn these responses from us.

To produce contentment we need to battle. These battles are not won in church, though church has its role. They are won through a family culture that minimizes covetousness, cultivates generosity and encourages trust.

16
GRACE
The Value That Saves Core Values

"Forgive, and you will be forgiven." LUKE 6:37

"Father, forgive them, for they do not know what they are doing."
LUKE 23:34

*"Bear with each other and forgive whatever
grievances you may have against one another.
Forgive as the Lord forgave you."* COLOSSIANS 3:13

Grace is not just one more core value. It is the salvation of the other thirteen. You may live by the most dedicated moral standards, incorporating them into your daily family life. If, however, you lack grace, these values will lead you into a blind alley.

I'm thinking of people who look back on their upbringing with revulsion. If you had seen their families years before, you might have picked them out as models for the rest of us. When other families were lackadaisical and lukewarm, they remained strict and disciplined. Yet the children, when they grew up, wanted nothing to do with that life. They found that it lacked grace.

Jesus never provoked such a reaction. He never compromised his standards, yet people flocked to him. "Sinners" invited Jesus to dinner—so often that he got criticized for it. (The Pharisees and the Bible teachers despised Jesus' indiscriminate friendships.) Jesus made great demands on people's lives, but they evidently didn't resent it. Instead, they were inspired by it. Grace does that, infusing core values with love and inspiration. Grace must do that in our families.

THE DEFINITION OF *GRACE*

Grace is one of those sweet-sounding words that people like but can't easily define. It slides in and out of different contexts, assuming a different shape in each one. Grace is not a "thing." Grace is an attitude and a perspective so basic that it transforms whatever raw material it touches.

The essential definition of *grace* is Jesus, especially seen on the cross where he gave his own self for the salvation of the world. While we deserved nothing but God's rejection (and the righteous glare of the outraged fundamentalist), we got instead the loving embrace of God. We were pardoned for our most shameful behavior, helicoptered out of the mud and flown directly to the warmest firelit celebration we ever imagined. "Amazing grace, how sweet the sound, that saved a wretch like me." That grace shapes all of the core values we try to live in our family.

Grace means believing in the best in each other. When you live with people, you get to know what they will do. You are quite ready for Jack to lose his temper, for Susan to disappear when there is work to do, for Phil to talk nonstop about himself. You expect them to disappoint you in the old familiar ways. Such expectations may be self-fulfilling prophecies. More important, such expectations drive away all life and hope. You feel the heaviness in the way family members talk to each other. You see in their eyes that they wait expectantly for you to fail again. Such attitudes fall on you like a heavy net.

We need grace to lighten those expectations. It may be illogical to overlook the past, but such personal faith is badly needed.

Many people remember some family member—a grandparent, an older sister—who believed in them and encouraged them at every step. I think of my mother. She surely knew my faults, but she always encouraged me, always expected me to do well. I wish I had a dollar for every time she said, "You look so nice when you smile." Me, the pimpled, scowling teenager! She saw what I could be and expected that I would be. I didn't thank her at the time, just scowled. Yet she kept on. That was grace, pure light falling from heaven—to have someone believe the best about me, day after day.

Sometimes grace goes in the other direction, from children to adults. I've talked to men whose lives began to change because they saw the adoring looks their small children gave them. When someone expects wonders from you, it gives you life.

Grace comes undeserved. It can't see the past but shines a light toward a wonderful future. Such grace can completely transform a person. Without it, all the family values in this book won't help people.

Grace obliterates bitterness. In *The Will of God as a Way of Life,* Gerald Sittser says that the past can hold us captive in two ways. First, regrets for our own failings can overwhelm our ability to live in the present. Second, bitterness over others' failings can sour relationships and prevent us from moving on. We grind our teeth over remembered offenses, and soon they completely dominate our thoughts.

My wife often counsels married couples in crisis. Quite frequently, one partner or the other brings up a remark that was made years before—sometimes many years. Often the partner remembers a cut regarding intelligence or weight. (The one who made it usually has no memory of it.) Bitterness has nursed that careless remark until it has grown into a monster.

It happens between parents and children too. Some people can't let go of family failings—of the father who never came to see school concerts, of the mother who left home and never came back, of the parent who never said, "I love you."

Grace speaks to regret and bitterness in the language of forgiveness. Sometimes we talk about forgiveness as though we understand it, as though it is a perfectly natural human interaction. Forgiveness is more like a miracle. How a person consumed by his own past failings can come to release them like helium balloons I do not understand. I see it happen, but I cannot explain it. How someone whose mind helplessly plays and replays a long-ago hurt can come to release the bitterness is beyond me. But it happens when grace touches their lives.

Failure is inevitable in families. Even wonderful families who incorporate core values into every aspect of life still fail. These failings, unleavened by grace, can destroy us. They can turn our excellent values into weights that crush us under their expectations.

Grace lifts these crushing weights; it transforms a family with joy.

Grace gives freely. We have mentioned God's extravagant love and the stupendous generosity with which he showers undeserved blessings on us. God gives freely. Usually, humans don't.

BABETTE'S FEAST

In his wonderful book *What's So Amazing About Grace?* Philip Yancey recounts Isak Dinesen's short story "Babette's Feast." This parable of grace has been made into one of my favorite films. It makes me smile but also weep at its extraordinary vision of grace.

The story is this: In a tiny, remote fishing village two sisters carry on the tiny church founded by their beloved father. Years have passed since his death, and the members have aged and grown quarrelsome. Then Babette, a refugee from the French civil wars, arrives. Babette says she was a cook in France, though that means nothing to the sisters. Out of kindness they take her in as their cook. They eat a tasteless Scandinavian diet, which Babette learns to prepare. For many years she does so, and though she always remains something of a stranger, she is dear to the two sisters because of her selfless service.

Then one day Babette receives astonishing news. She has won the French lottery, 10,000 francs. The sisters expect that Babette will return to France. But first Babette makes a request. She would like to cook the sisters and their church a French meal, at her expense.

Somewhat nervously the sisters accept; they have no idea what French food could be like. Babette prepares a fabulous meal, with incredibly rich sauces and sumptuous wines imported from France. Despite themselves, the members of the little church are warmed by the repast.

After Babette has cleaned up the countless plates, glasses, pots and bottles, the sisters approach her to say thank you. They also ask when she will leave for France. Babette shocks them by answering that she is not going back. Why? Because she has no money. No money? Where has it gone? She spent it all on the incredible meal.

Like the old woman at the treasury in the temple, she has given her all. Like the woman who knelt at Jesus' feet, she has poured out an incredible gift with no thought for the sensible or responsible. Babette, it comes out, was once renowned as the greatest chef in Paris. Through all these years she has labored to boil salt cod for the sisters, but in her soul she remained capable of extraordinary delights.

"But dear Babette," one of the sisters exclaims, "you should not have given all you owned for us!"

"It was not just for you," Babette says quietly.

"Now you'll be poor for the rest of your life!"

"An artist is never poor," she says.

Babette refers to an old friend, an aging opera star who had once met the sisters. "He said: 'Throughout the whole world sounds one long cry from the heart of the artist: Give me the chance to do my very best.' "

Given a chance to do her best, Babette gave everything she had.

So grace does. It is unfathomably generous. Core values will enable a family to live a good life, but sometimes that is not enough. The work of an artist, pouring out his or her best, goes beyond good behavior. Grace can save a family when nothing else will do.

Chapter ten dealt with submission, the core value that enables family members to accept disappointment while sustaining their trust that God will work out good. Grace goes beyond submission. It is active, not passive. Grace does not merely outlast disappointment—it heals it by pouring out its creativity and its generosity.

That sort of generosity will always be exceptional. You could hardly talk about it as "family culture." That makes it sound too routine. Nevertheless, some families do live gracefully and generously with each other. They don't merely accept each other's failings. They give so generously to each other, and to all, that they are healed.

Grace swallows pain, absorbing it. It is a rule of life that pain does not disappear. The classic example is the father who gets bawled out by his boss, comes home to yell at his wife, who throws her temper at her child, who kicks the dog. The dog then bites the mail carrier.

Any counselor will tell you that ignoring pain won't work. You will only internalize the hurt, becoming bitter, taking it out on others, or giving yourself ulcers. That happens in many families, including many Christian families who don't believe in fighting. Failing to express their anger overtly, they become stiff and tense, speaking politely while fury rages inside. In such cases, the other core values will offer little help. Only grace can heal.

Grace is not an attempt to shrug off the hurt, pretending it isn't felt. Grace comes from Jesus, who absorbed the pain of human hurt on the cross. At the core of grace is always his suffering and death, appropriated into our lives.

Those who grasp their forgiveness in Christ, and who understand the astonishing grace of Jesus in dying, can absorb the pain of others' hurtfulness. They do so not by ignoring others' hurtful behavior but by presenting it to God in prayer. In saying this I don't mean to suggest that they never confront the other person and try to resolve differences. In fact, they do. However, that communication has its limits. Sometimes people can't change, or won't. Grace goes beyond those limits. It takes the pain into itself and obliterates it.

Grace goes beyond our resources. It is the ultimate "God thing." We are not, of ourselves, able to do this. Only God can. We carry his grace into painful family situations and use it like medicine to neutralize the poison.

THE HABITS OF GRACE

Grace and forgiveness can become habits of family life. Rigid and punitive families can't even imagine letting go of regrets and reproach. Families attuned to grace, though, hear its sweet call sounding always. They listen for it and look for it; they hope for it.

The culture of grace usually starts with a parent, or preferably two, who exemplify its forgiving attitudes and hopeful expectations.

Parents ask forgiveness. If parents want to create a culture of grace, they must not hold grudges against their kids. They must forgive and forget their children's sins and absorb the pain of their wrongdoing.

Graceful parents must believe in their children beyond the evidence.

When parents humbly *ask* forgiveness, that goes to a deeper level. Inevitably it comes as a shock. Kids suddenly realize that their parents are human, and that they too need grace. What is more, kids suddenly find themselves in power. Grace is asked of them, and they are on the spot.

It may seem a small matter to ask forgiveness from your children. Parents make mistakes, after all. They lose their temper; they fail to listen; they misunderstand and jump to conclusions. Why shouldn't they ask forgiveness? Yet many parents find this excruciatingly hard to do. Perhaps that reveals the extent to which they do not really know grace. Why wouldn't they hope for grace from their own dear children?

Parents forgive each other. My friend Harold Fickett writes about his wife:

> Besides the fact that I enjoy her company and she makes me laugh, Karen's greatest strength and thus the greatest strength of our relationship is that we both admit to being wrong and sincerely ask the other for forgiveness. And we both do forgive each other.
>
> As you say, this is a miracle. But it's the miracle without which no family can live in any way that approaches happiness. If families are schools of charity in which we learn how to love, that means learning how to forgive and learning the power of forgiveness to breathe fresh life into what otherwise would die.
>
> A mom and dad with kids have every inducement to forgive one another. You look at the tots and think, "Can I really betray them by harboring this anger toward their mother that I know will not only hurt her but them as well?" It's possible but you really have to be hard-hearted to do it, and willfully blind yourself to the link between the mom and the kids.

When parents forgive each other, the whole family feels the influence.

Wipe up each other's spilled milk. I don't think anybody can raise a family without knocking over a few glasses of milk. Even parents do it occasionally. Children do it frequently, because they're small and weak and haven't gained all their coordination, and also because they tend to hurry.

I have seen a lot of milk spilled, but I don't think I've ever seen anybody do it on purpose. Usually the one who makes the mess is filled with dismay, perhaps even with shame. A small but powerful statement of grace is to clean up for them, without a word of reproach. In our family we make it a rule: nobody cleans up after their own accidents. Sometimes the parents do it, and sometimes another child is assigned the task. (They may grumble, but still they learn the expectation of grace-filled behavior. When they make a mistake, the same "justice" will be dealt to them.)

Make them shake hands. When children fight—as they usually do—they find it hard to make up. They get so furious, or so hurt, that they can't let it go. So parents separate them, talk to each of them and hope that time heals the wounds. Generally it does. Children are blessed to be able to forget. An hour or a day later they act as though nothing ever happened, and they go on as before.

The only trouble is, forgetting is not the same as forgiving. Sins "forgotten" may really be kept in some hidden corner of the mind, stored up for future retribution or rejection. Forgiveness should be explicit. It should bring the sin out into daylight and deal with it.

To try to prevent grudges, some families insist that children make up. They must say out loud that they forgive each other, and show it by a handshake or a hug.

Of course kids don't want to do this. Sometimes they are not ready to do it—they are still mad. Sometimes they are willing to forget about what happened, but not to make such an explicit show of it. (This suggests that the forgiveness is half-hearted.)

And of course, often when parents insist that their children "make up," the response is phony. They shake or hug, they say the words, but inside they are still fuming.

Even so, the effort shows that anger and hurt won't be swept under the carpet. If the parents' intervention doesn't always result in genuine reconciliation, at least it sets the stage for it by demonstrating that the parents expect it and hope for it.

Generosity to the homeless. Some of the most gracious people I know are astonishingly generous with homeless people. I remember sitting in an outdoor café with my friend Joe when a rather disreputable-looking homeless man shuffled up to us. I already had all my defenses up, prepared to bid the man a cold farewell. Joe, however, stopped our conversation, talked to the man and then went into the café to buy him an ice cream. Ice cream wasn't what the man wanted, it turned out, but I was amazed by Joe's willingness to be bothered.

I'm quite prepared to say that such generous behavior does nothing to help homeless people. Neither does donating spare change. Even taking a homeless family to the grocery store and buying them food is unlikely to prove a potent strategy for alleviating their poverty. The problems of the homeless are deep, and I am convinced we offer our greatest help by giving generously to agencies with skill and experience in helping them—groups like the Salvation Army or a rescue mission.

That said, generosity like Joe's does teach grace. Your children, especially when they are young, don't get to see you write checks to charities. They do get to see the way you react to people who are messed up and under the judgment of society.

Every family has to figure out how to respond to homeless people, and I doubt anybody has the all-purpose solution to their plight. I certainly don't feel confident that I'm ready to prescribe the right response to others. All I know is that I would rather be made a fool a hundred times than to have a heart of stone.

I also know that children watch carefully how we react to the homeless. The moment when they pass someone begging is very emotional to them. People like Joe, who respond with generosity and humanity—with grace, no strings attached—plant a powerful example of grace in the minds of their children.

THE STRUGGLE TO FIND GRACE

When I lie awake at night, my thoughts easily fall into a rant of bitterness or regret. Fears and recriminations boil up. I find anxious thoughts hard to lay aside. I have to work hard to pray with thanksgiving and love.

No wonder that in the daylight I find it hard to react graciously to someone who wrongs me, that I'm so ready to rebuff a homeless person, or that I can react punitively or sarcastically when my kids make a mistake. I need grace. I can offer to others only what I possess, and grace is not a constant in my life.

We cannot make ourselves gracious. Grace comes from heaven. We cannot manufacture it, no matter how hard we try.

We can, however, make ourselves available to grace. The old terminology, mostly forgotten, still applies: "means of grace." Prayer, worship and sacraments are ways for grace to enter our lives. Scripture, friendship and spiritual disciplines bring the grace of God to us. Through such means we show, in Kenneth Bailey's words, that we "accept being found." We accept that we belong, by God's grace, among a forgiven people.

The family culture of grace and forgiveness starts with the culture of Christ's body—with church. Of course church is a human institution, always mixing up grace with other less godlike qualities. Yet grace can always be found there, since Jesus promised, "I will build my church, and the gates of Hades will not overcome it" (Matthew 16:18).

This itself is a grace. Not only will God always give grace to those willing to accept it, he has tied that grace to a place we can find. We do not search for grace in dark spiritual mysteries. Grace has come to earth in Jesus; grace has come to earth in his body, the church. Grace is available, for us and for our families. That humanizes all the core values, giving them life.

A FEW FINAL WORDS
Putting Core Values to Work

*"It is for freedom that Christ has set us free.
Stand firm, then, and do not let yourselves be
burdened again by a yoke of slavery."*
GALATIANS 5:1

I very much appreciate the words with which Scott Peck began his influential book *The Road Less Traveled:* "Life is difficult." Until we accept this fact, Peck says, we will subject ourselves to great frustration. We will run in circles and tie ourselves in knots, looking for an easy and stress-free way to live. Only when we acknowledge that life is difficult can we discipline ourselves to make the most of it.

Not only is *life* difficult. *Families* are difficult. For every moment of nostalgia-splashed sunshine, we get five of dark fury, frustration and noncommunication. Parents struggle with their children, children struggle with their siblings, and Mom and Dad don't consistently get along. Creating a good family takes hard work. Nobody can do it for you. Nobody but you and your family members can pray the prayers that must be prayed; nobody else can guide the conversations to settle conflicts. You must do it yourself, and in your own way.

This book is meant to be a tool to help. I mean it to provide encouragement as well as a lot of good ideas how to build a family around core values. You, however, now that you've read it, must take it and put it to work. That is difficult.

TAKING INVENTORY OF YOUR FAMILY CULTURE

Each family will apply this material in its own way. Nevertheless, I want
to sketch an approach you can use. It begins with sizing up the unique-
ness of your own family.

Start where you are. Make a list of what your family is known for, of
what you like to do, of activities big and small that you try not to miss.
Going through the past year's calendar may prod your memory. Or try
looking through the photo album.

Then, next to each item, write down what core values get expressed
through that activity.

For example, sports are part of our family culture. If you ask our
neighbors to describe the Staffords, they will probably mention how often they see one of us going off on a run. They might remember back to
the many days when we played catch or kicked a soccer ball on the
street. But what values do sports express?

I can think of five: hard work, joy, family unity, contentment and submission. I want to consider how I can emphasize each of these values in
the realm of sports. Let me show you what I mean.

The first value is *hard work*. We need to support—not undermine—
that value. For that reason Popie and I have always emphasized that
practices are not optional. If our children become members of a team,
they attend practice whether they feel like it or not. They should work
hard and not mess around. Popie and I don't think that sports are fundamentally very important. We are not trying to drive our children to
succeed as great athletes. We emphasize taking sports seriously because
we want to underline the value of hard work.

The second value is *joy*. I don't know any experience more ecstati-
cally happy than playing well and winning a close game. We try to underline this by encouraging our children to savor the moment—to live
it up, to celebrate. I don't want them to draw the lesson that they
should be driven to win. Quite the opposite! I emphasize that if you
play sports long enough and reach your proper competitive level, you
will probably lose about as many games as you win. So take your victories and celebrate them! Joy is a moment-by-moment experience.

Enjoy victories for what they are, celebrate and then move on.

As a family we try to celebrate with our children, to show them the joy *we* feel in their experiences. (I've seen families that only emphasize what could have been better. They don't savor victories, because they only stress improvement. They miss out on joy!)

A third value sports can teach is *family unity and love*. We emphasize that value by showing an interest and by attending games. Families that enjoy sports together can greatly strengthen their family bond.

The fourth and fifth values that sports can teach are *submission* and *contentment*. Those values come with sports because athletic competition involves disappointment.

As a boy I cared so much about games that I often cried when I lost. You can imagine how well that went over with my peers! I had to struggle with my feelings. I had to learn submission to the facts of disappointment, and contentment with my level of athletic ability. Those are values I have used over and over again in life. They are very adult values, but I first learned them as a child in sports.

I want my children to learn the same values. For me as a parent, this requires not making excuses for my child, and not letting them make excuses either. As a matter of fact, the culture of sports underlines this value. It's bad form to say that you lost because of the umpire. It's bad form to complain that your teammates let you down. You lost because . . . you lost. Even when you try hard and play well, sometimes you lose. But sports are still fun. You can get over disappointment. You can submit to the facts of the score. And you can let yourself feel contentment in the fact that you had a chance to play.

I remember attending a soccer tournament with one of my sons. His team lost all three games, and the kids were naturally disappointed and grumpy. One of the other dads said something to his son that I have long remembered. He said it cheerfully but pointedly. "Hey, don't take it out on me. You got to come here and play three games of soccer. All I got to do was watch." People who understand contentment and submission don't make others miserable when they lose. They don't even make themselves miserable. Parents can gently emphasize this point.

If I were making a list for our family, as I suggest you do for yours, it would look like this so far:

Family Culture	Core Values	To Strengthen Value
Sports	1. Hard work	a. Don't skip practices. b. Practice hard, play hard.
	2. Joy	a. Always congratulate, celebrate victory.
	3. Family unity and love	a. Attend games. b. Get siblings to attend whenever possible. c. Give snack bar allowance to siblings.
	4. Submission 5. Contentment	a. Don't make excuses for loss. b. Don't complain about the referees. c. Discourage moping.

My sister Elizabeth's family enjoys sports too, but they're much more intent on music. All of them play and sing well, and they obviously love performing. I suspect music teaches their family many of the same values that sports teaches my family—hard work, joy, family unity, submission. However, they must strengthen those core values through music differently than we do through sports.

All the elements of your family culture—the activities you enjoy, the way you celebrate holidays, your relations with your extended family, your enjoyment of movies and television, your approach to school and work—can be analyzed in terms of what values are taught and how these values can be emphasized and encouraged. This analysis will sharpen the way you do what you do.

I'd encourage you to begin this exercise on paper. Brainstorm (together, ideally) some of your family's habitual patterns. Then, using the list of fourteen core values, try to work out which ones stand behind those habits, and what you can do to strengthen them.

WEAK LINKS AND BAD HABITS

None of the core values is optional. Every family needs all fourteen. Yet we all have blind spots, areas we tend to overlook. And we all have weaknesses too. Some families will find, for example, that they have no habits of rest. They never really stop, they are always going, and though they talk about being tired and stressed, they don't have any habits that put a limit on their work. If this describes your family, you need to brainstorm ways to develop a culture of rest. Read chapter thirteen again.

Or suppose family unity and love is a weak habit. Perhaps the family you grew up in wasn't close. Possibly the busyness of modern life and geographical distances have kept you from close relations with grandparents, uncles and aunts. You may need to develop some family rituals to add to your family culture. Reread chapter seven for some ideas.

On the other hand, some of your family habits should probably be considered for change. If "all have sinned and fall short of the glory of God" (Romans 3:23), it stands to reason that all families have cultural practices that should be reconsidered. Perhaps you always spend the day after Thanksgiving at the mall, but the shopping gives you a frantic, materialistic edge. Perhaps you love sports, but you're obsessed with winning. Perhaps watching TV squeezes out any kind of conversation and harms your family life. Even very admirable cultural habits can get twisted. If so, you need to change or eliminate some elements of your family culture.

SPLENDID VARIETY

Take this book, then, as a sourcebook. Everything in it has worked somewhere for some family, but that doesn't mean it will work for you. My main aim in writing has been to stimulate you to think about what you're doing. You shouldn't just drift along. Rather, become intentional about family life.

Along with that, I hope I encourage appreciation of freedom. Every family is unique, and that fact should give us joy. God has given us a splendid variety of family culture!

The greatest limitation I feel in writing this book is this: I only know a small slice of that splendid variety. I know that my own family culture isn't the only way. I've tried to collect examples of different approaches, but I've barely scratched the surface.

Because of that, I'd like to close with an invitation. Write to tell me about your family culture. If you know another way to express these core values, please write to share it. I'm looking for examples that others can learn from. Should another edition of this book be produced, I'll add the best contributions. Perhaps, through a joint effort, this book can become more helpful as the years go by.

Send your ideas to Tim Stafford, c/o InterVarsity Press, P.O. Box 1400, Downers Grove, IL 60515.

For a free group discussion guide to this book go to
www.ivpress.com/bookdiscussionguides